BUILDING
WINNING
PARTNERSHIPS

BUILDING
WINNING
PARTNERSHIPS

A Ringside View

HARI BASKARAN

PARTRIDGE

A Penguin Random House Company

To order additional copies of this book, contact
Partridge India
000 800 10062 62
www.partridgepublishing.com/india
orders.india@partridgepublishing.com

CONTENTS

1. ACKNOWLEDGEMENTS

Thank you Gautam Brahma, Kaninika Mishra, R Srinivasan and R Vaidyanathan for taking the trouble to go through the initial manuscript and giving me valuable feedback for improving the book.

Thank you also to the OSA network of Modi Xerox who cooperated fully in helping me document their stories and share their views and experiences.

Thank you to my former team members in Modi Xerox for their support in bring out this book.

in this book show how policies and practices normally associated with large companies can be very gainfully implemented in relatively small establishments.

Thank you, Hari, for the effort you put in to bring out this interesting book.

Prakash Nanani
Former Group Managing Director, Xerox India.

3. INTRODUCTION

The Outsourced Service Agents (OSA) Programme was launched in Xerox India in 1998. It was by far the most emotive, yet the most satisfying programme I have ever been associated with. I always think about it with a great deal of pride and satisfaction, driven by what I believe was a tremendous transformation in the lives of many of our service engineers. Yes, of course, some chose to drop out along the way, but some grimly kept going in spite of difficulties and limited growth. However, many went on to be successful entrepreneurs. Their experiences will inspire people of all ages to take a plunge into the unknown and lead lives of courage and entrepreneurship. These untried and untested young men, who can serve as role models, have successfully shown the path to an alternate and sustainable career.

I have used the real life experiences of thirteen of the early adopters of the outsource programme to illustrate some of the critical aspects of programme management and the manner in which the programme evolved. The case studies of the early adopters of this programme bring out several good practices that are essential ingredients for running a successful business. I have touched upon some of the behavioural aspects of programme management and service outsourcing that would be of interest and assistance to young managers, confronted with similar demands in their professional life.

Each of the stories covered touches upon the lives and family backgrounds of the early adopters. They make fascinating reading and a strong reminder that in the final analysis, it is the quality and fibre of the people that matters and their value system and ethics. It would not be out of place to say that this value system and concern for people and customers were honed in these individuals by the ethos and organisation culture of Xerox India (then Modi Xerox). The reader will see this strong bond with the company coming out in many of the stories.

The unique organisation culture in Modi Xerox has resulted in very strong bonds among the employees long after they have moved on to other companies. It is people once again who create this organisation culture and ethos. One remembers with great fondness the many individuals whose presence and values collectively created the institution that Modi Xerox was.

While they are very many such stalwarts, I mention here a few who stood out for me personally: Prakash Nanani, Khurshid Bandyopadhyay, UR Saha, Arvind Agarwal, PM Pai, Deepak Mohla, Atul Sobti, DP Roy, Sandeep Mathur, Brij Chandiramani, R Shekar, Vinod Gupta, Naresh Malhan, Suvir Ahuja, Arun Kapoor, Hari Balasubramanian, Pradeep Kapur, SA Chari, Swetharanyan, Cherian Kuruvilla, Sanjay Kapoor, Vineet Bhatia, Parikshit Bhasin, Rohit Gupta, and many more who made Modi Xerox a very special place. The list is endless, and I may be excused if I did not mention some very dear friends and colleagues.

These stalwarts created an organisation culture that valued openness and trust and an equal concern for results as well as people. It was the ethos that they created in Modi Xerox that led to a strong concern for our employees, as the OSA Programme was being rolled out.

A. Modi Xerox in Transition

Several path-breaking developments were taking place in the late nineties in Xerox and in the business environment in India. The tight import restrictions of the earlier decades had given way to economic liberalisation, and the world of document processing was shifting to digital solutions, including digital copiers and printers. The Xerox Global HQ saw greater opportunities in India. Till then Xerox India's business was relatively isolated from the rest of the Xerox world.

Xerox India's products had necessarily to be manufactured in India with a phased indigenisation programme. The relatively low scale of operations meant that production had to be restricted to a few chosen products. This led to the long life in India, of the 1025 family of analogue copiers, long after it was phased out in the rest of the Xerox world.

The ownership of the company was a joint venture with the Modi Group, to form Modi Xerox. Liberalisation led to the purchase of the

Modi Group shares in the JV by Xerox so that Modi Xerox became a wholly owned subsidiary of Xerox with its financial results incorporated into the Xerox Global financial results. The Xerox India business strategies and product profile was integrated into the Xerox global strategies.

The first decade of the twenty-first century saw rapid changes in Xerox India. The product profile shifted away from the analogue war horses, built around the 1025 family, to the digital range of copier-printers. The Rampur manufacturing plant was no longer considered necessary and was closed. The business model swung away from a predominance of the mid and low end products sold and serviced by direct on roll sales and service teams to a partner-led business model at the low and mid end with Xerox's own teams focusing on the niche high-end products and solutions. Xerox's on roll head count dramatically reduced.

It was against this backdrop that the service outsources operations was launched in 1998 and was fully in place ahead of the inescapable march of the new business directives.

B. Going beyond Outsourcing— When People Matter

Most outsourcing initiatives are all about productivity and profitability gains. There are, of course, areas where outsourcing brings in competencies that may not be available in the company and where it is not worthwhile to develop the same in-house. Also the collaborative nature of today's businesses calls for strategic partnerships and for capitalising on complementary strengths.

Service outsourcing of the type covered by the OSA Programme is about productivity and profitability. It is the preferred option when a company wants to concentrate its direct resources on the high-margin niche products and services businesses and leaves the rest to outsource or channel partners.

Our service managers knew this and so did most of the potential OSA partners, drawn from within the company. They were understandably unhappy that this was the inevitable direction the company would take. We were, however, successful in creating a life-changing opportunity for the service engineers and managers and generating a lot of interest and desire to participate in the programme. We changed a potentially demoralising situation into one of challenge and opportunity. The case studies in later chapters show how a supportive environment helped bring this about.

That people matter is at the core of my value system, and this would be the only way that I would drive such a programme in the era in which it was launched. I had the good fortune to have senior managers who trusted me and gave me a freehand to run the programme the way I wanted to. This, you can say, was the Modi Xerox way. As a team, we rose to the occasion and created a lasting institution, positively impacting the lives of very many people.

I would like to acknowledge the enormous effort put in by the programme manager at HO, Vaidyanathan; the field service heads Ajit Kewalramani, Farooqui, Siladitya, Arun Thakur, Ramchandran, Balakumar, Puneet Gargya, Surendran, Bhargav Mistry; the HO managers Balaji and PK Gupta and the training and quality managers, Kapila and Bijani. There were many others all across the management chain who played a significant and vital role in the roll-out of the programme.

Many of the ideas and practices introduced in the OSA Programme are now common practices in the industry across companies!

4. IN THE BEGINNING

The outsourcing of service operations required all stakeholders to come to terms with service through channel partners. Neither the sales team nor the service team was ready for such a move, and an enormous amount of communication was necessary.

The sales team was afraid that outsourcing would lead to loss of control of service operations and a decline in customer satisfaction. We assured the sales leadership that we would put in place strong monitoring and control systems that would not allow a fall in service delivery standards. An important part of the communication to all stakeholders was that the outsource service team would be built from individuals who have been trained and have a long track record of success in Xerox.

The service community was worried about the retention of their jobs. They were unsure of their future. How many of them would get an opportunity to be outsourcing partners and how many would not. They were also apprehensive of their ability to run a business venture. Copious communication, face-to-face meetings with teams across the country, and one-on-one meetings with opinion leaders all helped gain acceptance of the programme among the service community in the company.

Thankfully, the customer service leadership team appreciated the strategic intent of the programme and did a great deal to help service managers across the country to come to terms with the need and benefits of the programme. Without consistent and sustained communication across the chain, it would be difficult to successfully launch programmes that need to be implemented across a large and widely scattered workforce.

A personal management style of being inclusive in decision-making and discussion within the team, of all matters of importance to our operations, also helped. The entire Customer Support HQ team was fully aware of the proposed directions and contributed fully to the success of the programme. Inclusiveness in decision-making creates an atmosphere where everyone is a contributor and everyone plays his role to the best of his ability.

A. An Auspicious Start

At the Inauguration of Jammu OSA

Just after the launch of the programme, a group of us from Xerox travelled in a Tata Sumo from Jammu to Pathankot, Dharamshala, Amritsar, and Chandigarh in Northern India to inaugurate the OSA operations in those cities. We continue to harbour wonderful memories of that tour.

Meeting the first-generation entrepreneurs we had helped create and experiencing these infrequently visited cities and the nearby places of worship was a delightful experience. It was a feast for the senses to be treasured; the warmth and friendship shown to us by the young entrepreneurs and their families added to the experience. I sensed we were laying the foundations of a worthy movement and knew that I would carry these memories deep within me and revisit these places again to see if the promise that seemed evident then would be fulfilled.

Dharamshala was a quaint town, more so McLeodganj. We stayed in a simple but comfortable lodging where the rooms overlooked the snow-clad Dhauladhar mountain ranges, a beautiful sight to behold in the mornings. We visited the Buddhist Namgyal Monastery and saw a large mandala being made out of fine-coloured sand. Each of us received a pure white silk shawl, which I still have in my prayer altar. En route to Amritsar we visited the Swami Chinmayananda Mission, where the Swamiji's body is interned, and the Brahma Kumaris Ashram. At Amritsar, we visited the Golden Temple, and on the drive down to Chandigarh, we briefly visited the Radha Soami Ashram at Beas.

The places of worship and the ashrams had a lasting impact on me. The country side in Punjab was lush green, and we got to eat yummy stuffed parathas with blobs of butter on them and washed it down with tall glasses of lassie, at popular dhabas along the roadside.

At each place, we were warmly received by the OSA partners along with their family and team members. There was Sanjiv Gupta at Jammu, Sharad at Pathankot, Jagmohan at Dharamsala, Jatinder and Harpreet at Amritsar, and Kulbir Dogra at Chandigarh. All of them were enthusiastic about their new role as entrepreneurs, though their family members were apprehensive and needed our reassurance that all would be well for their sons on this untried path.

This visit also set the tone for collaborative working and review processes that encouraged transparency in all matters, particularly finances. It was made part of the collaborative partnership that their operations would be reviewed and audited at regular intervals. It was six months after the initial launch of the programme that operational audits were put in place. Till then, it was necessary for the fledgling entrepreneurs to settle into their new roles and for the programme managers to help them establish their operations in the most supportive manner.

We were always conscious of the fact that we were creating a partner network with individuals who had no background of business. Failure was not an option for us, and we did everything that we felt was necessary to ensure success of the programme. We owned the programme and took full responsibility for its successful implementation.

It was a time of new beginning for these families, and it was appropriate that we were immersed in spiritualism all through it. What is most heartening is that all these OSAs have continued to be associated with the programme and have grown to be successful entrepreneurs. Some of them have been featured in the case studies in subsequent sections.

Hari at inauguration of Jammu OSA

Ajit and Vaidyanathan at Jammu OSA inauguration

B. Protection of Earnings

It was necessary to induce the right people within the team, to opt for the programme. The late nineties was not the time for quick and ruthless roll-out of the programme. It was seen as a drastic step of leaving a prized job in a highly rated company and taking the risky path of entrepreneurship. It was necessary to win the confidence of the service management team across the country and to secure the agreements of the most appropriate individuals to accept the role of service outsource partners.

Most of the team members who went on to become OSAs had no background of running a business in their families and were first-generation entrepreneurs. We decided that the primary support for these early adopters would be protection of their earnings for the first year. This protection was planned to be phased out thereafter. This led to many volunteering for the programme. Today, such support for an outsource initiative would be most unlikely as outsourcing as a business model is much more prevalent and accepted. Nevertheless, I would always seek to find the support needs most suitable to the partners at the start of any outsourcing programme, as this leads to commitment and loyalty of the partners.

Most of the OSAs had a salary protection of approximately 1.5 times their last-drawn salary. The more senior managers who opted for this programme could not avail of such a protection, as the territories they managed did not allow for payouts for such a high level of protection. However, it is a tribute to the effort we made to gain acceptance of this programme that several senior managers opted to be outsource agents even when the level of protection was relatively lower.

Payouts to the OSAs were initially through compensation for staff they had to recruit on agreed productivity norms. This was the labour model used at programme launch. The ownership of the customer via the maintenance contracts was with Xerox, and all parts and consumables were supplied by Xerox.

The payout models, and in fact, the outsource model itself, would evolve over the years and eventually grow into the authorised service provider model, with the maintenance contracts in the name of the outsource partner and parts and consumables purchased by him. This migration was always the intent of the OSA Programme from its earliest days. A phased roll-out enabled the company to keep a tight control on the operations and also allows the partners to settle in comfortably into their new role as entrepreneurs.

A critical aspect of outsourcing is the transfer of ownership of maintenance contracts and hence customers to the partners. Companies need to put in place IT solutions that allow visibility of the service delivery to end customers and remain in touch with them, through effective customer relations efforts. Not to do so can seriously impact long-term business interests.

C. Programme Support

Service outsourcing in those early days was not very prevalent in the office automation industry. Xerox, and HCL, who were by far the leaders in the industry, prided themselves on having large on roll customer support teams. In the mid eighties when Xerox's market share was taking off in a big way in India, Xerox employed a fairly large proportion of graduate engineers as it was considered necessary for the service engineers to correctly represent the company. This was pruned down when it became clear that the attrition level of graduate engineers was far too high.

With declining margins for both sales and service in the mid—and low-end segments, outsourcing as a business model was introduced to lower the cost of operations. Service outsourcing gradually gained acceptance with the office automation industry. Many aspects of successfully managing an outsource service operation that we had put in place is as essential today as it was a decade ago.

Service outsourcing in Xerox faced huge road blocks, just prior to launch, from the sales team and from many in the corporate support functions. It would never have taken off at the time it was launched in 1998 but for the support of the senior leadership of the company. They knew that service outsourcing was a strategic imperative.

To win acceptance and ensure no fall in customer support standards, we had a strong team dedicated to the roll-out of the programme at the head quarters along with dedicated programme support managers at each region. We also had a dedicated technical support team located at every outsourced service location to provide training and technical support to the OSAs. A very high degree of audit and controls was also embedded in the programme structure though this was supportive in nature. Our intent was that this high level of support would gradually be weaned away as the programme stabilised.

The close and supportive connect of programme managers to the OSAs, in most cases, resulted in bonds that have lasted years after the OSAs learnt to stand on their own feet.

D. Family and Social Support

Enduring memories are beautiful gifts. I always recall with a great deal of happiness, the participation of family members in the

OSA Programme. An outstanding example was V Narayan's father N Venkatraman at Trichy and Madurai. Here is an edited version of what Narayanan's father had to say of his contributions to the operations in the MOSAIC magazine.

I am a retired official of the Tamil Nadu Government, having retired from service on attaining the age of superannuation. My son asked me to assist him in the business and appointed me as manager (admin). I am in charge of accounts and stores besides general administration.

It is a must that the OSAs have a completed and updated list of customers. The list is being updated regularly with details of names, addresses, phone number, status, etc. The new machines are added immediately so that we can canvass for service contracts.

A mini store consisting of spare parts, which are essential and frequently required, is being maintained. We maintain the stock keeping records meticulously, and so far there has been no variations found in the Xerox India weekly/monthly audits. The timely supply of spares to the field has kept our engineers in good humour and have led to achieving better results.

Receipt and allocation of calls are the most important items of work in the OSA operations. Planning is necessary in the allocation of calls so that calls received in a day are closed on the same day in city and at least on the next day for outstation calls.

Double entry mercantile system is being followed in maintaining the accounts. Three sets of documents are being maintained: the day book, ledger, and cash book.

Much of this may seem mundane. However, what is noteworthy here is the participation of a parent in the programme and the meticulous manner in which he went about his tasks. Retaining process discipline is one of the prime requirements of an outsource operation. This is an aspect of outsourcing that is often overlooked by programme managers. Process audits enable transparency in the partners operations.

Stories such as this abounded in the early days of the OSA programme and added a new dimension to the family lives of these pioneers. This is something that moved me a lot. In the hectic lives, we lead in the corporate world, the family often takes a back seat, and most often the families are not made a part of office life.

E. Cashing in on a Heritage

Organisations of repute have a training calendar with mandatory training programmes and a fairly exhaustive portfolio of useful training courses. Programmes with the greatest value have training embedded in the day-to-day work. By this, I mean that the training programmes focus on the skills and tools necessary to support day-to-day operations and have an institutionalised system of facilitation and review in the course of daily work. This was true of the Xerox Leadership through Quality Programme (LTQ) that established the quality movement in Xerox in the late 80s and 90s and led to Xerox earning the title of the American Samurai.

The LTQ programme had at its core rigorous training conducted by excellent trainers, for each family group, that is, a manager and all employees reporting to him. Topics covered among others were meeting principles, communication skills, problem-solving skills, etc. In problem solving, we understood the importance of defining and agreeing to the problem statement, something that seems obvious but in practice, group members are left groping with different perceptions of the actual problem. After establishing what is the problem, then going on to where is the problem, since when and how grave is the problem, etc, backed by data analysis leads on to likely causes of the problem; the Five Why Method helps establish the Root Causes.

Likewise, we were trained on recognising the next-in-line customers and the importance of understanding the 'customers' specifications' and establishing 'suppliers' specifications'. A process of two-way communication between 'customer' and 'supplier' that establishes a mutually accepted understanding of all deliverables for the task on hand, at the very beginning, and ensures completion of the task right the first time. All these look mundane, but look around you and see how frequently these simple rules are flaunted, leading to rework and wastages.

In Xerox, the classroom training was continually reinforced by a network of quality specialist groomed from within each team, who ensured all meetings and group work followed the LTQ principles. Every manager was expected to be a role model in application of the LTQ principles and was, as a practice, reviewed by his manager in the application of quality tools in the course of his work.

Such a regime enabled the quality principles to be ingrained in an employee's work habits and was not restricted to just the quality network.

In fact, operations managers often turned out to be the most proficient in the practical use of quality tools.

> I credit this regime of training in Xerox as the foundation on which the adopters of the OSA Programme grew to be successful entrepreneurs.

Likewise, the training programmes around the self managed work group (SMWG) programme, for the service engineers and managers, was grounded in the tools and processes required of a self-managed group to function effectively in day-to-day operations. Managers of SMWG teams were taken through an intensive programme titled manager as a quality leader, a programme designed to convert a manager from being control-oriented to a facilitator of self-managed teams. Team members were taken through a programme called very appropriately in Xerox UK as 'Hot Housing' and just 'Team Development Programme' in India and were trained in tools they would use in empowered work groups.

As in the case of the LTQ movement, the SMWG movement dramatically increased the quality of the work and enabled team members to be groomed for higher responsibilities.

> In retrospect, the SMWG movement turned out to have far-reaching impact on the lives of the employees, and many of them went on to take positions of responsibility not just in Xerox but in several other companies in the IT, office automation, and telecom sectors. I would go on to say that this programme too was the foundation for the successful transition of many service engineers to entrepreneurs.

Such is the power of training embedded in the work way.

F. Applause from the Captain

The first issue of the OSA News letter MOSAIC dated July-September 1999 has the following article from the then head of operations Dr Naresh Malhan.

Dear Colleagues,

In a short span of six months, the Service Outsourcing Programme has exceeded all expectations. A large measure of this success is on account of the structured manner in which the programme was unfolded to employees. My heartiest congratulations to our service teams at Head Quarters as well as all the Customer Business Units located across the country for their excellent contribution to the Programme.

Outsourcing as a concept was introduced in Xerox India nearly a decade ago when we pioneered the Indirect Channels of Sales in the industry. Today Channels has grown into a vibrant family, over 350 strong and contributing close to 50% of our total sales. It is an invaluable member of our extended family.

We are ready to add yet another new member to the team— Out-sourced Service Agents. The outsource programme is here to stay. Apart from being a key enabler to enhancing productivity, the Customer Service Teams have shown that it can be a vital business opportunity. Outsourcing promotes the entrepreneurial spirit across the company. Our aim is to offer new opportunities that will unleash more such success stories across Sales and Control functions besides Service.

For those of you who plan to embark on this momentous journey in your careers, I urge you to focus on the four pillars of entrepreneurship:

Manage your People

It is people who build organisations and make them successful. They are a vital asset. Value them. Your success as an entrepreneur depends on their commitment, motivation and support.

Manage your Money

Successful entrepreneurship rests on business efficiency. Ensure your operations provide adequate returns, focus equally on both the money you earn as well as that which you spend.

Manage Yourself

As an entrepreneur, the responsibility of motivating and energizing your teams for superior results rests on your shoulders. Keep your own spirits high and sustain high motivational levels across teams, in your business.

Manage Excellence

Maintain uncompromising focus on excellence. Inspired leadership and excellence are the twin pillars to success. Drive your teams to excel in all they do.

I have every reason to believe that Xerox India has provided each employee tremendous opportunity to imbibe and gain knowledge even as we strive to grow. My best wishes are with each one who is embarking on a new exciting journey that unravels your entrepreneurial skills

With regards,
Dr NK Malhan
Managing Director
Marketing Operations

As always, Naresh has very sound advice for all of us. His four pillars of successful entrepreneurship is so well put and so very apt. I am sure many of our OSA partners will appreciate the wisdom of this advice when they reflect on the journey they have been through.

Speaking of success, just how successful was the OSA programme for Xerox India? My association with the programme was from 1998, its inception to early 2003 when I left Xerox India; so I will restrict myself to the benefits of that period.

Customer Engineer Head Count reduced from 676 to 142.
Outsourced workloads increased from 36 to 480 Field Managers reduced from 79 to 23
Field technical support manpower reduced from 64 to 35 HO Manpower reduced from 18 to 6
Annuity revenue per effective head increased by 20 per cent
Productivity per effective engineer increased by 17 per cent
Service labour to annuity revenue reduced by 2 per cent
Customer satisfaction increased by 2 per cent

5. ON THE RUN

It has been a fascinating journey for me as I interviewed one on one, thirteen of the early adopters of the OSA programme from across the country. In all the cases, I could capture their family situation and background along with their journey as entrepreneurs.

In choosing the entrepreneurs to include in this book, I have been guided by the need to cover the early adaptors across different geographies in the country and also to have a fair selection of those who broke away from the Xerox fold and those who stayed with Xerox and those who dropped out as entrepreneurs. As part of the selection process, I sent a questionnaire to as many of the early adopters whom I was able to connect with through email. The quality of the responses and the willingness of the partners to participate in a venture of this nature narrowed the selection further. Thereafter, it was a question of selection based on the learning that could be derived from the experiences of the partners without it being overly repetitive.

It was fascinating to see how each entrepreneur carried into his organisation the training and values he had imbibed at Xerox. This is a tribute to the Xerox training and development programmes of the past. There can be no better testimony to this than their voluntary implementation into one's own company. It was no wonder that Xerox's training and development programmes of the past were considered the best in class. It is unfortunate that in recent times there seems to be a marked reduction in these initiatives.

From the early protected days, the OSAs have had to learn to cope under tighter financial terms and greater investments in the business. This has been a struggle for most of them; however, they found the answers, mainly through cash flow and expense management and micromanaging the business. This, simple as it sounds, is the most important differentiator between successful and unsuccessful businesses.

Programme management from Xerox changed over the years, as indeed it should, from tight controls to a more arm's-length approach. Overcontrolling an outsource programme defeats the very purpose for introducing the programme. However, as the programme matures, it becomes necessary to evolve into a collaborative mode of working. The paternalistic controls of the early days needs to shift to a more mature supportive style as the partners settle into their businesses.

Xerox has faced steep erosion in service revenues and significant losses to its customer base that indicates operational errors along the way. The experiences of the OSAs, as narrated in the subsequent sections, bring out some of the shortcomings of programme management over the years. I have highlighted some of the critical issues that play a part in the successful management of service outsource operations.

A. Entrepreneurial Streak at Work

The first four case studies bring out the nascent entrepreneurial streak in some of the OSAs. These early adopters were clear in their mind that they wanted to run a business of their own. They were quick to adapt to the changing needs of the programme and looked beyond the captive Xerox business. Once they were on the entrepreneurial road, there was no stopping them.

BS Arunkumar's story is atypical of the other OSAs. He clearly displayed the desire and ability to run a large business from the very beginning. The OSA programme was the ideal start for him on his entrepreneurial journey, although in many ways his journey commenced much before the OSA programme. He had a dream, the spark that ignites entrepreneurship. Arun recreated in his company the environment that moved him so much in Xerox. He put into place the empowered work groups and the customer satisfaction initiatives that Xerox was well known for. His story is unique for his ability to create an energised workplace and retain his employees, a difficult proposition for relatively small companies. Attempts by the local management to build alliances with other sales partners is an example how local concerns can create mistrust and doubt leading to the loss of key service partners.

Ramki and Ravi Dhale displayed clarity of purpose and decisiveness—the hallmarks of good entrepreneurship. Ravi very thoughtfully created a brand around his company that spelt reliability and trustworthiness to his customers. You could say that in the office automation arena, he was the king of Kolhapur. He realised that he needed to grow beyond service outsourcing, if he has to remain profitable in a small town such as Kolhapur, and reinvented his business to build a business around providing brand agnostic solutions to his customers.

Ramki's risk-taking ability can be seen from the gambles he took with high-volume sales and the investment in a Canon Imaging Store. The short-term interests of the local management team once again resulted in the loss of a strong partner. What also comes out in his story is the trust deficit that grew between him and the company that he was so very fond of. Openness and trust are the essential features of outsource operations, and the leadership team of the company needs to go out of its way to built this environment with partners.

BNC's story is remarkable for his resilience in the face of difficulties. One often sees the hand of destiny in the lives of the intrepid. His story also brings out the need for transparency and end-to-end visibility across the leadership chain, to avoid conflict of interest issues, and the need to be fact based in performance assessment and in rewards and punishments. Implementation of policies at the ground level is critical for the success of any programme, and ethical values must never be compromised by either the partner or by the local managers.

1. A Successful Transition to Entrepreneurship

Ramki at office gate

Ramki was the very first to be associated with the service outsource programme and ran one of the two pilots that was set up for management of the routine maintenance operations. This was then spun off as the first phase of the OSA programme that included routine maintenance and low-skilled breakdown calls. His decision to shift out of Best and Crompton and join Xerox India twenty-one years ago was preceded by a very interesting episode. His father wanted him to join the TVS Group, where he had worked. Best and Crompton offered to almost double his salary and give him an out of turn promotion to stay on. Ramki wanted to join Xerox. It was decided that the names of the three companies would be written on slips of paper and a draw made in the presence of the deities in the family's prayer room. His father suggested three draws, and the choice would go to the company with the majority picks. The Gods ordained that he should join Xerox and so it was that all the three picks went in favour of Xerox!

Excellent management of a remote location leads to selection as an OSA

It was Ramki's dedication and successful management of all aspects of a remote location, Hosur, which caught the eye of his service managers. His management of customer service operations, collection of debts and service contracts, and his ability to pick up machine sales orders, due to excellent relationship with customers, were held up as benchmarks for other remote locations in the country. It was not surprising that the service management team in the South, Balakumar and Rafeeiudin, offered him the OSAship. It was a very good choice and for Ramki, a life-changing decision.

> A key success factor for a service outsourcing programme is the right choice of partners. This is not the avenue to get rid of difficult or undesirable employees.

He adapted very quickly to the life of an entrepreneur and has significantly increased his net-worth. From the humble start of a loan of Rs 1.50 lakhs from a friend to start his operations, he quickly moved to an overdraft facility with his bank, supported by collaterals in the form of property papers. His instinct for business and confidence in his ability to manage sales operations led him to take aggressive calls on bulk purchases of machines at favourable prices. He was soon not only a trustworthy OSA but also one of the largest sales partners for Xerox in the country and the distributor for Tamil Nadu.

By 2010, his relationship with Xerox had soured, and he broke away to join Canon as a sales and service partner. He currently also runs a Canon Imaging Retail store at Trichy. True to his eye for detail and fact-based decision-making, he has gained an understanding of a domain new to him, retail sales management, and is doing well. Canon would very much like him to open another retail store in his home town, Madurai, which he plans to do after he fully establishes the Tiruchi Outlet.

Trust deficit leads to the loss of a partner

So how did Xerox allow such an achiever to leave and join a competitor? The answer has lessons for effective programme roll-out and partner management. When Xerox wanted to hive off its low-end photocopier business, it chose to transfer the large machines in field (mif) to the OSA under the authorised service provider (ASP) Programme. The ASPs were required to take over the mif and the outstanding debt on payment of a fee, which for Ramki was Rs 10 lakhs. He had to continue paying the technical service fee for his territory at Rs 2.50 lakhs and like all other ASPs had to purchase spares and consumables exclusively from Xerox. Ramki didn't believe that Xerox had done the right assessment of his territory, and his appeals for review of the active mif and revenue potential fell on deaf ears. He and other ASPs were offered a take it or leave it choice. He took it and incurred considerable losses, as most of the debt couldn't be collected and the revenue projected by Xerox was way off the mark.

To add insult to injury, Ramki was induced to lift a large quantity of machines to meet year-end targets of the Xerox Sales team; and in the very first week of the new financial year, Xerox announced the appointment of Redington as the National Distribution Partner. This made it difficult for Ramki to sell stocks to re-sellers. After a struggle for over three months, he finally managed to clear stocks. Xerox had refused to take back any of the machines they had thrust upon him, prior to the announcement of the National Distribution Partner or provide any support to him.

This is an instance of lack of transparency and trust affecting the relationship with a strong partner. As the programme matures, the need for transparency and openness assumes important proportions. High handedness results when managers place outsource partners as lower in the pecking order. Close interactions with partners all the way up the managerial chain avoids the buildup of trust deficits.

These short-sighted actions by Xerox led to Ramki breaking away and joining Canon where he once again made a mark for himself. Successful outsource operations whether of sales or service must always be carried out in an atmosphere of openness and trust and above all fair play.

Ramki's social standing climbs

Business acumen apart, Ramki is drawn towards serving society and is today a worshipful master for the Freemason Society in Chennai. He champions three socially relevant projects supported by the Freemasons: providing decent burials for the unclaimed bodies of the destitute lying in government hospitals, providing artificial limbs for the disabled who can't afford them, and supporting an orphanage in the outskirts of Chennai.

His net-worth has considerably increased, thanks to judicious investments in land and property and is today worth several crores. He proudly took me around his house at Mugappair in Chennai, designed and constructed to his tastes and that of his daughters. His daughters, Niveta and Monica, have grown up to be confident and accomplished young ladies. Both of them won their way through competitive exams to a prestigious visit to the NASA Facilities in the US and also to the Albert Schweitzer Programme for Leadership Development at Ireland.

What are Ramki's mantra's for success?
* Constantly reviewing his options and seeking new avenues for growth
* Realising that service outsourcing alone was not enough and he needed to be a successful sales partner as well.
* Strong belief in ethical work practices that won him the support of the principals he worked for
* Always seeing the positive side in all relationships

As Ramki was taking me around his office, he showed me a large pile of machines reclaimed from customers under trade in schemes and felt it was occupying too much of valuable space. He believes he should clear this space and set up a demo centre and copy bureau. With a State Bank of India Branch opening nearby, he feels the walk-in customers will be high and the per page rates are attractive these days. That I guess is the spirit of entrepreneurship.

> If there was one piece of advice I would offer to Ramki, it would be that he should be more circumspect and evaluative when he pitches for excessive stocks, either to please or to gamble.

With daughters Niveta and Monica

2. Building an Energised Workplace

Arun at the inauguration of his new office

From the day Arunkumar stepped into Xerox in 1987, he was extremely happy with the supportive environment and the training and development opportunities that were provided to him. He was conscious of the fact that he came from a humble background and the team in Xerox seemed way ahead of him. He would return from service calls every day, carrying copy quality test charts, and would discuss the performance of each machine and all that he had done during each of the calls with his seniors. They in turn would give him useful insights into the performance of the machine and what he could do to get better copy quality.

He devoured all the inputs given to him, just as he had done at the Indian Institute of Science, where he would go for evening classes. He enrolled for a wide range of courses, while he was employed at an electric motor manufacturing unit, in the Peenya Industrial Estate in Bangalore. The company paid him a paltry sum of Rs 350/- per month and he had several opportunities to move to better paying jobs, all of which he refused. He was more interested in the tremendous learning opportunity the company offered him and the experience he was gaining in all aspects of running a business, from product development to sales and marketing and production engineering.

> Arun had invested several years of his initial working career into self and technical skills development. His days, more often than not, ended well after midnight, without dinner and an hour long walk back to his place of stay. This investment in development is something one sees lacking in many young professionals.

While having a performance-oriented culture, Xerox provided a family environment and lots of encouragement, besides training and development. For Arun, this was an unimaginable work environment, and he gave of himself wholeheartedly to the tasks on hand. Arun refers to this phase as the golden period of his life.

Arun introduces Xerox's team development programmes into his business

The LTQ training, the problem-solving techniques, and the SMWG programmes were all dear to his heart, and he not only absorbed them but made them an integral part of his work and leadership ethos. As he would say, it was in his blood.

In all his future endeavours, he would replicate the work culture he experienced in Xerox and the emphasis on placing employees first. He incorporated the best of the Xerox processes and style of operations into Accura Solutions, including the customer-focused activities, the use of customer voice forms, adherence to meeting principles, and the SMWG work way. Even now, every week, three groups—Thunders, Matrix, and Popcorn—hold regular meetings and conduct monthly reviews. The groups recognise the star of the month for individual performance. Other initiatives include conducting regular knowledge-enhancing training programmes and picnics with family members.

Here is an excellent example of incorporation of a work ethos that leads to employee engagement and retention. These essentials are often missing in proprietary firms and the stumbling blocks for growth of the business.

Openness and trust are values that are very dear to him. Likewise, equity and fair play are the bedrocks on which he would build his future companies and the primary reason for his success.

The seeds of entrepreneurship are sown in Arun

While he was in the electrical motor manufacturing company at Peenya, he believed that there was a large market for permanent magnet motors. These were being imported, with high-import duties making them expensive. Arun was of the opinion that these motors could be made locally, at much cheaper rates. While the owners of his company appreciated his point of view, they were not keen on business expansion, or in making the necessary investments in capital and time to build this product line.

Long after he left the company, Arun continued to have a strong desire to make his vision come true. Late into the night, after his stretched working hours at Xerox, he would work on a design for a permanent magnet motor. He would use simple techniques such as manual winding and an electrical stove to bake the armature, as he struggled to build a working prototype.

He finally succeeded in making a satisfactory prototype and placed the details, along with a photo of the product on several leading magazines, including, *Industrial Product Finder*, *Electronics for You*, etc. He was overwhelmed by the responses he received. Having clearly established the potential, he induced two of his friends to collaborate with him in setting up a manufacturing unit called Magna Motors.

He would provide all the technical assistance, while the other two would run the day-to-day operations. Arun was emphatic that he didn't want to leave Xerox, and the help and support he provided for the manufacturing project was late at night, when he had completed his responsibilities for the day in Xerox.

Managing partnerships

Arun's work ethos extended to the management of his partnership. None of the partners of Magna Motors have left him from inception till date. By mutual understanding, they would ploy back all profits into the business, but each year, they would decide to purchase a household gadget, the same for each of their families. One year they gifted a gold chain to each of their wives, and in 2000, they each purchased a plot of land, valued at approx Rs 3.50 lakhs, on the company's account. The plots were purchased at Sahakar Nagar, an up and coming colony along the road to the new airport. Today, this property is considered one of the prime areas in Bangalore where Arun has a wonderful house that he meticulously constructed as per his taste.

> This is an outstanding example of equity and oneness of mind among partners in a business. The ability to work together over long periods of time calls for a clear understanding of roles and responsibilities (what each one brings to the table) and transparency and mutual agreements on how the surpluses from the business are shared.

In 1999, Arun grabbed the opportunity for taking an OSAship at Bangalore. He was extremely keen on replicating his Xerox experience. He provided the same supportive environment for his employees and spent time and effort in their grooming and development. His wife also took an active role in the new company, Accura Solutions, and reached out to each employee. They grew so close to her that whenever they needed any help or guidance on the personal front, they would first of all connect with her and take her guidance.

In 2006, when the ASP model was being rolled out in Bangalore, some of the local Xerox Managers tried very hard to get Arun to partner with the existing sales dealers Binary and AB Value Point. Arun refused and said he would take up the ASP on his own. His detractors tried to make out a case that Arun did not have the financial strength to be an ASP. He took up the challenge and offered to put in as much funds as Xerox considered necessary for successful operations. Arun then went about setting up a benchmark office, on the lines of Xerox or any other company of repute. He took on rent a spacious office that could house forty-five or more employees, in Rajaji Nagar. He furnished the office with a reception, a work control room, separate rooms for each of the three work groups, and separate office space for the accounts and admin staff. His stores even had moveable racks, just as there were at the Xerox warehouses.

Office rents even in those days were high. Arun paid Rs 28,000 per month as rent on a five-year agreement. He anticipated that there would be a threefold increase in rent thereafter. He has since purchased a plot of land in Sahakar Nagar and has built an ideal office. He conducted a grand inauguration for the new office in 2010, where the employees participated as if it was their own office.

Employee first initiatives enable benchmark retention

The employees were given special awards for long service. Those who completed five years were given a silver trophy and a cheque of Rs 5,000 along with a letter that went to their parents. The family was also invited out for dinner. The ten-year long service employees received a silver trophy and a ten-gram gold coin, and the wives were given a sari. The family was also invited out for dinner. In the fourteen years since he has set up Accura Solutions, six employees have stayed with him since day one, five have been with him for over five years, and he has no fresh employees in his current team size of twenty-four. Such was his track record on employee retention that Xerox invited him to Delhi to share the best practices he deploys for achieving such high levels of employee engagement and retention.

Arun has spoken to three of his key employees that three years from now he expects them to have an equal stake in the business as he has and that he will groom them to take over the running of the company. He has pledged to develop his team members with this aim in mind.

> Sadly, Xerox has not been able to retain Arun and Accura Solutions as a business partner. Arun says that he was gradually getting disillusioned with the new work ethos in the company. The old caring attitude was missing, and there have been negligible development inputs. There seems to be an excessive concern for the short-term and a vast gap between the field realities and the directions that the head quarters were issuing. The local teams also had agendas of their own, at times at variance with the central directions.

Here, we see that there is no appreciation at the local management of the damage that the loss of a strong partner can cause to the business results of the company. Mature handling and a partnership approach is essential.

There had been a steady decline in the profitability of operations and Xerox's directive to take over the loss making Kohaku machines finally led to Arun deciding to part ways with Xerox. True to form, he placed the matter before his team members and shared financials and the expected losses that Kohaku would bring. The team was of the unanimous view that they should reject the proposal from Xerox and if asked to exit the business, Accura would surely find other takers.

> This is an example of insensitivity to a partner's financials and lack of a mature dialogue based on trust and openness. The cost of losing a strong partner is often overlooked when authoritarianism is the mode of engagement. This is where mature partner management is required.

Arun exits the Xerox business

There were several other takers for Accura, as by now the company had earned a name for reliable customer service in the market. Arun eventually chose Konica Minolta. It is ironic that the local leadership team of Xerox was critical of Arun's selling ability and his lack of focus on sales. As against monthly sales of three to four colour copiers that he sold when he was with Xerox, he has now sold over 160 Konica Minolta copiers, including several colour copiers, over the last eight months. Clearly Konica Minolta is out selling Xerox, in that market. To add to Xerox's woes, approximately 50 per cent of the customers have preferred Accura's services and moved over to them, seriously eroding Xerox's service revenue in that market.

Arun plays a lead role in his community

Arun is a man of many passions. He championed the cause of the 'Basavabalaga' movement in his colony. This is a movement that offers support to his Lingayat community, when they need help. They also conduct regular monthly meetings called 'Thingala Thilihu' (new knowledge). Arun has created a blog covering these activities: [http://www.shreebasavabalaga.blogspot.in/].

In these meetings, experts in various fields deliver lectures that are enriching to the members of the society. Over 300 families now attend these monthly meetings which have been running non-stop for 125 months.

He also writes a blog, which is devoted to the family deity 'Shree Verabhadreshwara, son of Lord Shiva'. He has carried out extensive research and has identified 1,100 temples and shrines dedicated to the deity in Karnataka. He has visited 150 of them and has written about each on his blog along with photographs:

[http://www.shreeveerabadra.blogspots.in]

This is truly an exceptionally scholarly effort that Arun is putting into his blog. Arun is also interested in astrology and is currently studying the astrological indicators for childless couples. This would certainly be a much sought-after research study.

Here is the advice that Arun has for budding entrepreneurs and young professionals:

❋ Focus on the basics and be meticulous; embrace into your way of working anything new that you learn.

❋ Believe in people development, delegation, and the personnel touch with everyone. Be sensitive to their feelings and be supportive.

❋ Be ethical, honest, and have confidence that you can win when you are in the right direction.

❋ Respect human values. Believe in God and have the blessing of your parents.

❋ Have a dream and work for the long-term; don't opt for short cuts.

---

3. Clarity of Purpose and Deliberate Choices— the Road to Success

Ravi receives an award

A life-threatening accident shapes Ravi's life choices

It was on 27 December 1988, four days before his marriage and just a year with Xerox, that Ravi met with a life-threatening accident. He was a pillion rider on a motorcycle, along with a sales colleague from Xerox while returning from a sales call in Sholapur, when the motorcycle suffered a puncture and the two of them were thrown off the bike and rendered unconscious. To their good fortune and by the grace of God, a passer-by took them to a nearby hospital from where they were transported by an ambulance to Kolhapur, their base location. Ravi had suffered haemorrhage in the brain, and he was in a critical condition.

On reaching Kolhapur, he was rushed to a neurosurgeon who decided to immediately conduct an operation to remove a blood clot that could be fatal. The operation could not be performed immediately due to a power shutdown. Family and friends of Ravi rushed to the power station and cajoled and browbeat them into restoring power on an emergency basis. Thankfully, the operation was timely and successful and the clot was removed. Ravi regained consciousness after thirty-eight hours, and his cognitive abilities were in order; he was, however, bedridden, and it would be several months before he would be in a position to get back on his feet.

The parents of his bride-to-be were justifiably concerned and felt the marriage, then just a few days away, should be aborted. They took a doctor along with them to discuss the matter with the surgeon who had performed the operation. The surgeon told them that Ravi was now out of danger, but there was no certainty on how long his recovery would take and the extent to which he may be disabled. The girl's parents were of the opinion that the marriage should be called off but to her immense credit, the girl insisted that the marriage (which incidentally was a traditional arranged marriage) should go on as planned. The marriage was delayed till 14 February 1989 (it was not widely celebrated as Valentine Day then) when he could just about participate in the ceremonies; thereafter, his wife nursed him back to health till he was finally back on his feet, after almost six months. All through this tough phase, Xerox stood by him taking care of most of his hospital and treatment expenses until Ravi got back to work and gradually resumed his usual taxing routine.

It was no wonder then that Ravi felt that his place in life belonged at Kolhapur, where his wife and parents were most comfortable. For him, whatever would be the fruits of success in his professional career must be made available to his parents and wife in full measure. These considerations would be the focal point of his decisions regarding his career.

Ravi's early experience hones his work ethos

Ravi's parents were not educated, as his grandfather was a freedom fighter who was most often away from home and undercover. Ravi did his schooling in Kolhapur and then B.E. in Mechanical Engineering from Walchand College of Engineering, Sangli. While his schooling was free of cost, he took a loan to be able to pay for his college education. On graduating from engineering college in 1983, Ravi got a job in a foundry in Kolhapur. It is here that his work ethos was established, in a result-oriented and hard working environment where people were disciplined yet happy. He names his manager, Venkatachalam, as his able mentor and guide in those formative years.

The foundry, however, closed down in three years, and Ravi secured another job with Thermax in Pune in the Design and Applications Group. It was a job that Ravi disliked and decided to leave after just a year. After a few months of being idle at home, he secured a job as a customer service engineer at Xerox to be based at Pune.

Success in Xerox opens career options

In Pune, Ravi threw himself into the new job, thrilled at the salary he was getting and excited by its challenges. He was often sent to very tough and demanding customers, as a form of ragging as he would say; however, he managed his customer relations very well and earned praise from customers and his sales and service colleagues. After a period of a year or so, he was posted to Kolhapur to cover the vast and scattered territory of Western Maharashtra. He worked extremely hard and soon won the loyalty and full satisfaction of the customers in his territory. He was considered the role model engineer in terms of productivity, customer relations, and all other service parameters.

In 1994, he was promoted as a customer service manager at Kolhapur after his complete recovery and rehabilitation from his life-threatening accident. Ravi arguably won the maximum number of awards by any person in Xerox in those days. This included the weekly and monthly contests, five grand slam events, 100 per cent customer satisfaction score in three consecutive surveys, and so on. Ravi was enamoured by the professional work environment in Xerox, which was result-oriented with transparent and practical performance measures in place and strong and effective feedback mechanisms.

In 1999, the OSA movement was launched, and Ravi was given the option of moving to Mumbai or Pune or any other metro. He decided against any of these moves and opted instead for the OSAship at Kolhapur. His performance and standing within Xerox would have led to upward mobility in his career and the prospects of reaching the higher echelons of leadership. However, this was not what Ravi was seeking, and he preferred to remain in Kolhapur, a decision that could have meant stagnation and career frustration.

In the first phase as an OSA, he was comfortable and fully engaged with the process of setting up the office and in training and developing his team. The performance of the location and his management of operations continued to win him praise and confidence of the Xerox service management. Post-2002-03, he began to feel uncomfortable with the future directions of the OSA programme and had differences of opinion with the way the territory of Western Maharashtra was planned to be run.

Xerox had initially divided the territory into several manage—able geographies with OSAs in each of the locations. Now, there was a move to consolidate the OSAs, and Xerox encouraged Ravi to take the leadership in a unified outsource partnership for Western Maharashtra. Ravi didn't want to take the lead responsibility in this partnership, nor did he want to serve as a member of this alliance. He felt that short-term considerations would prevail, and he suspected that the ethics of business that he considered non-negotiable would be violated. In 2003, he resigned as an OSA and sought avenues of business outside Xerox.

Ravi reinvents his business model

There were several organisations that approached him to be sales and service partner, and this included HCL and Canon among others. He chose HCL, as the office automation division of HCL offered him a wide product array outside just copiers. He did well for HCL and secured business in excess of what HCL was hoping to do in that territory. However, in course of time, he was unhappy with the levels of support HCL was providing and their policy of going directly to the customers in competition with their partners.

Ravi would try other companies, including Sharp. However, he found the situation not very different from his experiences with HCL and concluded that a location like Kolhapur was a small and insignificant territory for most companies and the level of support or the attention of policy makers of any company would be low.

He decided that the best way forward for him was to be a solutions provider and a systems integrator. He would use his considerable personal brand equity to get information on a customer's requirements and then agree on specifications before offering products from any manufacturer who best suited the requirements. He was extremely particular about long-term benefits for the customer and proving them the right level of both pre-sales and post-sales maintenance support. This was a winning formula for Ravi, and there has been no looking back for him since then.

This is a very good example of clarity of purpose and goals in re-inventing ones business. Clarity of purpose is often missing in an entrepreneur, leading to his or her business stagnation or wrong choices in the quest for growth. Ravi also shows that a business can be made successful even in a relatively low-potential territory. His decision to be a solution provider backed by strong customer loyalty is unique among the OSAs.

His net profit from his business is more than adequate for his requirements, and he sees no need for business expansions just for the sake of growth. He runs a hassle-free operation and has extremely high loyalty among his customers. Today, his company is once again the leader in the office automation business in Kolhapur. His wife is a strong supporter and business partner who looks after the order placement and financial transactions with the principals and receivables from clients.

Ravi has led a life of his own choosing, on terms that he would not comprise on, and has succeeded. He has finally found the time to further his interest in classical music and has enrolled for singing classes.

Ravi's advice to young professionals is

* Make business a win-win for all constituents. Principals have the technology and their own strategic vision. It is the entrepreneur who implements the company's plans and wins the loyalty of customers.
* Take the long-term interest of customers into account at all times.
* Ensure that your employees' protection and well-being is your responsibility.
* Remember that money and fame are not the only yardsticks of progress.

---

4. Unflinching in Values and Ethics

BNC and wife Mili

Entrepreneurial training under difficult circumstances

BNC's father passed away in a tragic drowning accident just one day before he was born in 1953. His mother then had the uphill task of bringing up her four children, with nothing but the merge earnings their modest farm and livestock brought them, in a village near Dum Dum airport in Kolkata. A year later, a raging fire destroyed their home. A kind village elder had given her money, which BNC's father had left with him for safe keeping, and this was used to rebuild a two-room dwelling. Those were the days of going barefoot to school and eating just one meal in two days.

His father's sister helped, by bringing up first the eldest son and later BNC, through their schooling. BNC moved over to his aunt's house when he was in class 6 and stayed on with her till his schooling was completed. While schooling was free, BNC earned modest sums of money by providing tuition to younger children, to fund purchase of books and other essentials. He earned Rs 10-Rs 20 per month from these tuitions.

On completion of schooling, he studied BSc in Kolkata. Classes were infrequent, so he and a few friends set up a small school for needy children in thatched accommodation. Within a year, the student strength reached 400, and teachers were six unemployed youth. The schooling was free, and the only source of income was through private tuitions that brought in Rs 80-Rs 90 per month. Books and other requirements for the school children were provided free by NGOs Nir-ahkarata duri Karan Samaity, a wing of Calcutta University student circle. It was here that BNC would imbibe the rudiments of running an establishment, however small it was.

Kolkata was then under the threat of the Naxal movement, and with the increasing militancy of unions and poor power situation, most companies exited Kolkata, and jobs were exceedingly difficult to come by. BNC felt he needed to study further and enrolled for a four-year diploma in Electrical Engineering at the Jagdish Chandra Bose Institute in 1975. For BNC, college was just a necessary evil and a means to a livelihood. He did not appreciate what this education would bring to him and preferred to spend most of his time running his school and managing attendance at the diploma course though proxies provided by friends!

When he did make an appearance at class, he would be quizzed by teachers who didn't recognise him as a student. It was one of the teachers, Prof. Samaresh Mukherjee, who took him aside and told him of the world that awaited him if he completed the diploma creditably. He also explained that the government was spending Rs 4 lakhs per student for providing these facilities and it would be a waste if he took his studies so casually. He asked him to think things over for two days and speak to him again or leave the institute. This made a very deep impact on BNC, and from that day onwards, he concentrated on his studies while his friends took care of the school.

In 1979, he completed Diploma in Electrical Engineering in the First Division and secured a job in Kolkata, with a firm K Dhandapani & Co who were distributing household and office equipment. However, in just twenty-eight days, he received a job offer from Kores India and was posted at Cuttack, initially as a service technician and then as a sales and service technician. His interest in the xerography technology took him to Xerox India (then Modi Xerox) where he eventually applied for a job and was selected. In both these early jobs, BNC performed to the full satisfaction of his managers and was highly rated. Xerox, however, would be the turning point of his life and the platform for the future course of his life.

Xerox the turning point in his life

In Xerox, shortly after BNC had joined, there was a big move to get engineers to take remote postings. Bob Ashcroft had made a strong plea to influence engineers to take these postings, and there were attractive incentives offered. BNC had preferred to remain in Kolkata; however, one of the engineers who had initially opted for Bhubaneswar backed out due to family pressures, and BNC was induced to go in his place on the promise that he would be brought back to Kolkata in a year.

In 1989, he was subsequently asked to take over the position of commercial engineer at Rourkela. BNC did brilliantly at Rourkela and was declared the best commercial engineer in the country and received many gifts from the company in kind besides incentives. He honed his sales and commercial skills during this posting which would serve him in very good stead later in his career as an OSA and an independent entrepreneur.

BNC had offers to move to sales in Xerox and also to take up a customer service manager's position at Bhubaneswar. He decided to take the CSM position and moved back to Bhubaneswar in 1990. He was to stay on at Bhubaneswar and then took up the OSAship in 1999 at the same location. In the meanwhile, he earned laurels for himself that took him to almost every Xerox grand slam event and gave him the opportunity to see exotic places such as Paris, Kuala Lumpur, Bali, Amsterdam, and many more. For a person with such a humble background, this was quite amazing. As BNC would say, it was through the grace of God.

He led Bhubaneswar for three consecutive years as the best of the best branches. His long stint at Bhubaneswar also enabled him to develop a strong rapport with his customers that would be most useful during his innings as an entrepreneur.

BNC opts for OSAship

BNC opted for the OSAship for Bhubaneswar in 1999 on a labour model for the first two years, which was then revised to labour plus material on a revenue sharing model. The terms were tight, and he had to manage his affairs with strict control on costs and cash flows. He just had a couple of lakhs in his bank account but availed of the loan of Rs 1.50 lakhs that Xerox offered him and also benefitted from the provident fund accumulation of Rs 3.50 lakhs that was released to him. He managed his operations with the flair and result-orientation that was always his hallmark.

Far-sighted and pragmatic decisions, strongly supported by his wife Mili, ensured financial security for the future. While still an employee in Xerox and subjected to frequent house changes, due to landlords wanting to secure higher rents every year, BNC found an ideal solution by taking a house on rent cum ownership basis. With a down payment of Rs 60000/- and a monthly rent of Rs 2,500/- he would pay for the house in fifteen years. Xerox agreed to stand guarantor, and he was the proud owner of a flat in 1994. Post taking up the OSAship in 2002, he wisely invested in office space of 1,200 sq ft in a commercial complex close to the airport, after taking a loan from LIC Housing Finance that was available for SOHO owners. He also utilised money received from the sale of ancestral property to invest in a 12,000 sq ft plot of land at nominal costs that has appreciated several time over the years and against which he has now come to an agreement with builders to construct a housing complex.

BNC's shrewd investments brought him financial security over time. This is a necessity for those seeking the entrepreneurial way and with the usual clutch of responsibilities of taking care of the family and settling the children. Most of the examples in this book have shown that this financial stability is achieved through judicious investments and is a natural corollary of business growth.

Lack of transparency opens the way for malpractices

Things took a turn for the worse for him when, BNC claims, a corrupt manager in Xerox demanded that he pays him Rs 5 lakhs for renewal of his OSAship. BNC was shocked by this turn of events and spoke to his wife about it. While he could have made the payment demanded, he was inclined to refuse and face the consequences including loss of the OSAship and the resultant financial burden. His wife agreed that they should firmly decide not to make any such 'slush' payments. The manager levelled allegations of mismanagement of the operations and financial irregularities and harassed him on every little issue, including delays in executing spares orders and delays in payments.

At some stage, an auditor was sent to conduct a field audit, and he reported the use of a third party selenium photo receptor by one of the technicians. This was seen as grounds for serious malpractices, and on the advice of the manager, even without adequate consideration of his position, BNC's OSAship was terminated in July 2003.

In such matters, it would seem like one person's word against another. However, subsequent developments proved that serious injustice had been done to BNC. On the advice of well-meaning friends in Xerox, BNC, and another OSA sent a formal complaint to Xerox senior managers alleging irregularities and wrongdoings by the manager. Xerox took serious note of the complaint and had the same investigated fully. The manager was charged with malpractices and dismissed from service with immediate effect.

> The bane of most programmes spread over vast geographies is differing quality of implementation at the field. All such programmes need to be backed by regular field visits by managers across the hierarchy and regular reviews by the senior management at the partners' location. This results in transparent operations and keeps a check on local programme implementation and management. Remote management is far too costly in the long run.

BNC rebuilds his business sans Xerox

Back in Bhubaneswar, BNC decided to try hard and find new business opportunities. The local sales manager of Xerox sought his help in closing a large deal for a DC 470 printer/copier at Kalinga Institute of Technology (KIIT University). The director of the institute suggested that BNC should purchase the machine and provide print and copy services to KIIT. BNC agreed to this, and with the help of a bank loan of Rs. 10 lakhs, he purchased the machine from Xerox at Rs 13 lakhs and signed a five-year contract with KIIT.

Meanwhile, Xerox finally settled all his dues and far from having to pay to the company Rs 4 lakhs or so, he received Rs 7.8 lakhs from Xerox as unpaid dues. He used the entire amount to clear a substantial portion of the loan he had taken from LIC HF. Renting out 1,000 sq ft of the office property he had procured in 2004 and retaining only 200 sq ft earned him Rs 35000/- pm.

He was now financially stable and above all had gained immense peace of mind. His regular visits to the Ramakrishna Mission in Bhubaneswar and his active participation in the discourses of the Katha Amrita were a source of solace. The copy and print shop he had set up at KIIT was an extremely rewarding change from the perpetual tension and nit-picking that he had to face during his OSA days. He was then always under the beck and call of the Xerox managers who treated him as an outsider from whom the maximum had to be extracted.

In 2009, KIIT University wanted a complete renegotiation of the contract, and BNC lost out to another party who offered a much cheaper Canon solution. But by this time, BNC was considerably wiser and mature in handling moments of crisis and uncertainty. He used his extensive contacts in Bhubaneswar to set up a chain of copy shops located in educational institutions and has been running the same with the help of on-site operators. Today, he is gradually transferring these copy shops to the operators so that they can earn an independent livelihood.

The boy, who had no money to buy a pair of slippers, now was an enlightened person who knew the source and well spring of absolute happiness and sought to be of service to others through his association with the Ramakrishna Mission and in the pursuit of a vision to establish training facilities to help undergraduates be more employable.

His advice to young professionals is
* Be ever hungry for success
* Be honest and sincere in your efforts at all times
* Be tenacious and battle through the difficulties of life.

Vijay and his wife Renu

5. Battling Adversity

Vijay's migration into the world of entrepreneurship seemed ordained by the Gods. Almost as if they held a gun to his head and urged him into it. Just as his wife, Renu's uncle had literarily held a gun to his head and ordered their marriage to be conducted the very next day!!! Many things in our lives indeed are moved more by destiny than conscious choice. Vijay's story is not one directly related to the OSA programme but as his training and background was very similar to the OSA partners, his experience bears sharing in this account of entrepreneurship.

Many dates are etched indelibly in Vijay's mind, as is his date of joining Xerox India on 17th July, 1984, after he had completed his Diploma in Electronics from the Pusa Institute in Delhi. He had missed getting into Delhi College of Engineering by just two marks but that certainly hasn't effect his career and fortunes very much. He recollects how hesitant he was at the interview conducted by Bob Ashcroft and Raghumurthy. He struggled to speak in English and had often to break into Hindi!! You would never guess that when you see how fluent he is in English now.

It was just after his confirmation that he was posted to Lucknow, and on his very first day there, still grimy from the train journey, he met a distinguished gentlemen at the restaurant where he was grabbing a quick breakfast, who walked up to him and asked if he was the new service engineer and asked him to go along with him immediately to the Chief Minister's office to install his photocopier. Vijay managed to get some time to freshen up before he dashed off to the CM's office for the installation. The distinguished gentleman turned out to be Dr BK Modi, the President of the company!! The installation turned out to be of a 1045 photocopier, something that Vijay had not been trained on. Undaunted he went ahead and successfully completed the installation and was duly patted on the back by Dr Modi.

Many laurels and memorable events were to follow, none more path breaking than being summoned at short notice to attend an Assessment Centre. Apprehensive and unprepared as he was and grilled over several days with case studies and presentations, he caught the eye of the assessors and was given a high rating. He was appointed as a Service Manger, the youngest in the company at 25 years, and posted at Bhopal where he performed creditably and consistently over several years.

In 1995 he decided to leave Xerox and took up an assignment first with Sriram Refrigeration as the National Service Head and after a year, with Gillette to head the Braun Products service for India and South Asia. Both were learning grounds for Vijay. At Sriram Refrigeration he understood the need for cost effect service operations and helped set up the service agents programme. In this programme approx 35 service employees were encouraged to take up the programme as entrepreneurs. He also introduced a unique mobile van operation for compressor replacements at the customers premises. The seeds of entrepreneurship were being sown within him gradually.

Likewise in Gillette he introduced a partner friendly spares strategy where the auditing and claim settlement was through a third party agency. So well accepted was the programme that a senior Philips Business Manager called him for discussions and besides congratulating him on the spares strategy also offered him a job!! The service operations of Gillette were almost completely outsourced with even the warehousing handled by logistics partners. The appreciation of partner enabled and cost effective operations would stand him in very good stead when he moved into his own business operations.

The hand of God was soon to strike. In 2002 he was called to the Braun Headquarters in Germany and there he came to know that Gillette would be hiving off the non shaving products and the Braun service operations in India would soon be wound down. The Gillette India management suggested that he take up a National Distribution partner assignment and also offered him a fairly lucrative VRS package. After much deliberation and in spite of his wife's misgivings, he decided to accept the offer. Friends and well-wishers helped him take the decision, with Surendran being a major influencer.

He was also tipped off by friends in Xerox to meet Bhuwan Khulshestra, who was then the Programme Manger for the X'Mart Programme in Xerox India. This was a programme to refurbish traded in photocopiers at the Rampur Factory and sell them through an alternate distribution channel. Vijay made a strong case for himself and was appointed as one of just two wholesalers for this project. He was to handle North and East while RP Aggarwal was to handle South and West.

The Gillette national distributorship and the X'Mart opportunity were the ideal platforms for Vijay to commence his entrepreneurial life. He pragmatically set up a warehouse cum office in a modest basement, which his wife wept on seeing. She was understandably worried by the toll it would take on his health and well being. On 29th June 2002, his 40th birthday and another day etched in his mind, he resigned from Gillette and formally accepted the national distribution partner agreement. By mutual agreement it was only in the end of 2002 that he finally started his entrepreneurial innings.

Vijay's cost effective approach honed by the slim margins and profitability of the refrigeration and personal care product lines saw him establish a very lean set up. He just had four service engineers and an accounts assistant to manage the Gillette operations while he handled the X'Mart business all on his own. It was his strong appreciation of partnerships that enabled him to establish a sound working relationship with OSA Partners who were allowed to resell the X'Mart machines. He also made a significant breakthrough in forging effective working relationship with the Daryagunj wholesalers to widen his sales outlets. Very soon he had a thriving business with close to 50 to 60 X'Mart machine sales per month.

Running a lean operation required trimming all costs. Vijay worked on a deal with the Daryagunj wholesalers to pick up machines in lots of ten. This was the optimum lot for transportation and he arranged to have the machines transported from the Xerox factory at Rampur to the Wholesalers directly without any handling costs enroute and at the most optimum transportation costs. As he would say, the Darygunj partners didn't understand the language of the Leadership through Quality programme but understood the language of money.

In entrepreneurship one has always to expect the improbable. In 2004 came the news that his operations with Gillette would be wound down and within just a week of this jolt came the news that Xerox was closing down the Rampur Plant and the X'Mart operations would come to a grinding halt. It was a double body blow. To add to it, Vijay's business partner in a retail venture, Sandeep Kapoor, an OSA Partner wanted to exit the retail business. Vijay and Sandeep in partnership ran two Airtel retail outlets, one at Vikas Marg and one at East of Kailash, which were largely managed by Sandeep. Vijay asked Sandeep to continue for another three months while he worked out what exactly he wanted to do.

As can be expected the body blows had a huge impact on Vijay's health and lead to sleepless nights. When word of the closing down of operations reaches the market, partners clamp up on payment of dues. The struggle to get back receivables would go on for a very long time and eventually significant sums would be written off. Vijay was put on medication which the doctors said would be administered strictly for one month to avoid addiction.

In desperation Vijay decided to return to the corporate world and secured a job as the national service manager for Bright Point. But the Gods had other plans for him and a few months down the line at office, he felt discomfort and a severe headache and rushed to the hospital where the doctors were amazed that he had managed to drive down on his own. They treated him immediately for extremely high blood pressure and after a couple of hours he was out of danger. A full check up revealed no major heart related complications; however he would henceforth be on medication to keep his BP under control. At this stage Vijay decided that he would not gain very much from remaining in the corporate world and resigned from Bright Point to return to entrepreneurship.

In 2005 after careful thought Vijay decided that the only business he would be in would be the retail business. He knew that he would have to own the premises if the operations were to make business sense. He gave up the show room at East of Kailash and with the proceeds, purchased a showroom near his house at Vaishali. He also took up the East Delhi distributorship of Godrej Refrigerators and ICICI Small Ticket Loans as an interim measure till his retail initiatives were stable. He put in major efforts to ensure that the Vikas Marg outlet turned profitable. By 2008 he had generated sufficient surpluses to purchase the Vikas Marg property and exited the Godrej and ICICI businesses. He would thereafter concentrate only on his chosen line of telecommunication retail sales.

Now at the age of 50, Vijay has a feeling of gratification of a life well run. Of successes and achievements he is justifiably proud off. He now spends a lot more time with his family. He and Renu travel on outings together frequently and his focus is now on seeing that his children are well settled. His daughter, Apoorva has completed MBA from Lancaster University and is currently working at Aegis and marriage for her is high on Vijay's agenda. His son, Nakul is studying MBA at the Leeds University. He has the comfort of a sizable net worth built up through judicious investments in property and feels no major risk to leading a comfortable life.

Vijay's attributes his success to:

1. The blessings of his parents and the strong value system they gave him
2. The strong foundation he received at Xerox and the learning at all three companies.
3. The support and good wishes of his close friends and his life partner, Renu.
4. Taking life's decisions on the bases of his own strengths and weaknesses.
5. Knowing that he had God's blessings and guidance at every stage of his life.

Here's what Anuraag, the then GM of Gillette and one who played a major part in Vijay taking to entrepreneurship, had to say on Vijay completing ten years of entrepreneurship . . .

"Hi Vijay, Time flies and here we have a very successful entrepreneur. You are an inspiration to many; you did not give up despite all odds, continued to give the best to your children and continued to be deeply rooted in humility. Please congratulate your wife who has been a very strong support to you. Wish you continued growth and success. Best wishes, Anuraag."

B. Staying the Course

For many of those who opted for the OSA programme, it seemed an inevitable turn of events. They had a strong preference for the cities or towns they were living in and didn't want to relocate. They could see stagnation, in so far as their careers in Xerox were concerned, and the entrepreneurial option seemed an acceptable alternative.

The favourable terms of engagement, in the early days of the programme, and the degree of protection they received made it much more acceptable. What stands out about all these stories is the staying power and determination to ensure protection of their livelihood. This is particularly true of **Jatinder** and **Jagmohan**. Having tasted blood, so to say, Jatinder is now restlessly striving to grow his business. Jagmohan has built a healthy balance between his work and family and prides himself on the quality of his life.

Mitesh has the enviable ability to get the best out of any circumstance, and his affable ways wins him wide-spread support. He successfully managed the relationship with a financier, which is often the stumbling block in business partnerships.

Prashant has managed his business very much on the lines of well-established business houses and has applied the processes and practices that one normally associates with them. He says with pride that he has been able to attract people from larger established companies to join his company.

Saravanan has shown an astute business sense in monetising customer satisfaction. He has built on his excellent customer relations to convert many of them, to the advance payment terms, Volume Based Service Agreement (VBSA). This ensured that he was one of the few OSAs who didn't face difficulties on account of purchase of debt, when Xerox transferred the ownership of the machines to its partners. His approach to excellent customer relations is that every person in his company must treat all customers with the same respect and empathy that he shows them.

You can say that **Kulbir** learnt the hard way what it takes to run a business efficiently. Support from a business partner, that is rarely seen these days, and micromanagement of his business enabled him to come out of a very tight situation, and now, he is a confident and self-assured businessman.

No programme can be successful without the active participation of the leaders at the regional level and their dedication and drive to make the programme a success. Ram played a crucial role in programme implementation in the West and also in forging a partnership that took over the ASP role from Godrej in Mumbai. He went on to be the ASP for Nasik and has successfully extended his career through the service outsource option.

1. A Multifaceted Life in a Multifaceted Arena

Mitesh

Mitesh Dave was born on a leap year, 29 February 1972! It is, however, the manner in which he has led his life that makes him special! He has been decisive when it came to the crucial moments of his life and has been undaunted by uncertainty as he chose the path less traversed.

Mitesh was determined to lead his life on his own terms. He had met and fell in love, in school, with the girl who eventually would be his wife. He was certain of this no matter what the opposition from either of their parents. And marriage eventually took place in 1995 with the consent of his parents but without the consent of the girl's parents. They had a civil marriage in a court.

Failure in the second year exams of his diploma in Instrumentation Engineering was a critical turning point for him. He realised that his desire to be independent and self-supporting could only happen if he did well in his exams and secured a good job. He recommitted himself to learning and has been an avid student all his life. During his working days, he went on to complete post graduation in Marketing Management from Welingkar Institute of Management, an Institute with a good standing for the quality of its education, and then went on to complete a doctorate in Management with dual specialisation in Customer Relations Management & Entrepreneurship management from the National Institute of Management.

Mitesh displays versatility in Xerox

Mitesh was always seen as a high-potential employee in Xerox, and while he showed a flair for the technical aspects of his job, he was also very good on the commercial aspects and adept at building and maintaining good relations with everyone. He was amiable yet pushy and result-oriented when necessary, and, as we have said before, he had a mind of his own. Mitesh was a person with good all-round abilities.

He quickly moved up to be a senior engineer and then was made a specialist engineer for the new range of high-end copiers (5065F) that was soon to be launched. When the SMWG programme was launched in Mumbai, Mitesh was the most vocal at the training programmes conducted by Chandramouli, the programme manager. He instinctively took to the SMWG way, and it has remained as an integral part of his management philosophy. He became an SMWG Work Group coordinator in Mumbai, and later, when he moved to Delhi, he was the Work Group coordinator of the tech support and head office teams.

The influence of the SWMG training and movement can be seen here, just as in the case of Arunkumar. The SWMG approach trained service managers to be less control-oriented and more facilitator-oriented. It also trained them on the fundamentals of working with teams and resolving conflicts within teams. These traits broadened the approach of the service managers and were enablers for success in their future roles as entrepreneurs.

He was handpicked to move to H/O at Delhi as a product support manager for the 5065F copiers. At the head quarters, Mitesh describes the period from 1997-2000 as the golden period of his life, because of the immense learning opportunities he had both in technical skills and in the non-technical skills. He grew as a professional immensely during this stint in Delhi. This was also the period of the rapid digital transition that was taking place in the Xerox product range, and it required a complete re-skilling of the technical support team and the engineer workforce assigned to these products.

Mitesh opts for the OSAship

In 1999, the OSA programme was taking off, and Mitesh saw this as an opportunity to get back closer to his roots and his parents. Mitesh selected Surat as his preferred OSA location, purely on the grounds that it would be reasonably close to his parents, just 80 kms or two hours by train. Surat itself was a small location which he had never been to before, but this did not deter him.

> He had taken his decision on the basis of family considerations and that was it for him. Being decisive in decision-making is a necessary trait for all professionals and more so entrepreneurs. From the earliest stages of his life, Mitesh displayed this trait.

Mitesh took up the OSAship in Surat in March 1999 and initially stayed at his parents' home in Ankleswar. This meant that his day would start at 6 a.m. and end at around midnight every day. The service situation at Surat was in shambles. Apparently, the engineers of that location had not taken kindly to the OSA programme and the overall service situation had deteriorated to alarming levels.

The West Region Head had entrusted Mitesh to set right the situation in two months flat. With a 70 per cent population of jobbers spread out over a radius of 100 kms as his customer base, along with several very large and important corporates, Mitesh had his hands full. However, he went about it by meeting the customers and re-establishing faith and trust in the service operations with the support of the then service manager of Xerox, Aditya Chile. This meant extensive travel and hard work to get the machines back in good serviceable condition, besides meeting old commitments.

Hard work and sincerity always pays off, and soon Mitesh had been able to completely reverse the situation in Xerox's favour. The customer satisfaction survey (CSMS) for that year gave Surat a 100 per cent score with 71 per cent very satisfied! A score he would repeat in the CSMS next year also.

The situation in the joint family at Ankleswar grew unacceptable, and Mitesh and his wife and son moved to Surat to set up home on their own. This emotional break shattered Mitesh from inside, but he took it as just another challenge to establishing his business.

Initially, they stayed in the office itself, making it an office cum residence, not having the resources to rent out a house in addition to the office. Whatever funds he had was ploughed into the business and getting the office ready.

This move to Surat, however, benefitted the staff members because now Mitesh would start the day at 7 a.m. with training sessions for his fresh and under-trained technicians. Mitesh's love for continuous learning spilled over into his desire to provide training and learning opportunities for his staff members.

Success does not come without hard and dedicated work of the type that Mitesh put in at Surat. Young professionals are sometimes in a hurry to avail of the fruits of success and don't put in the effort that earns them rewards.

Two years after he moved to Surat, an opportunity came his way in 2001 to move to Mumbai as an OSA, and he decided to shift as it would lead to better prospects for his business. Moreover, he had his own house there and would not need to rent a place to stay. But there would be challenges a plenty that he took in his stride. He was given the territory of Central Mumbai from Prabhadevi to Andheri East, and his team comprised of employees culled out from the other OSAs. As can be imagined, the most difficult and least experienced of the lot was transferred to him!

Forging a partnership with a financer

In 2007, when Godrej exited the Xerox business, Mitesh joined Dhanpal Parikh of Elegant Stationers and Mansing Mohite, who also ran an OSAship in Mumbai. In a deal brokered by Ramchandran, the service head of the West Region for Xerox, Mitesh merged his company, Neil Enterprises, into the new company Technosoft Electronics Pvt Ltd in partnership with the others. Dhanpal Parikh was the principal financer, and the agreement was that two of his sons would join the company as working directors. This was an arrangement that required a lot of maturity and the ability to give and take in the right measure.

Mitesh managed this relationship comfortably, and the company thrived. This was due, as Mitesh acknowledges, to Dhanpalbhai's belief in maintaining both employee satisfaction and customer satisfaction. When Mitesh explained the need for investments or customer-related spends, Dhanpalbhai would readily agree. Mitesh also willingly consulted and took Dhanpalbhai's advice on all financial matters. That the arrangement worked well can be seen from the relationship continuing to date.

> Mitesh managed this perennially tricky relationship admirably. The relationship between a financer and an operations head needs to be cultivated in a mature and objective way. Often the relationship flounders on issues relating to command and control and inadequate dialogue. When both sides accept the relative strengths and weaknesses of each other and seek to use the strengths of each for the good of the business, a healthy working relationship is established. The financer is a critical enabler for an entrepreneur to achieve his dreams, and the entrepreneur needs to ensure that the relationship works favourably.

Technosoft started its operations from a large godown which had little or no facilities for an office. Gradually, the office was built up starting with the call centre which till then was run by Lawkim, the company which was providing these services to Godrej. Office infrastructure, cabinets and all other infrastructure would be put in place over a period of time.

The early months were a time of extreme financial stress. The burden of purchasing the debt lay heavily on the company. Godrej, in the months before exiting the business, starved the field of consumables and spares adding to the financial burden as over 700 machines needed immediate consumables change after Technosoft took over. With all the challenges, Mitesh and his entire Technosoft team outperformed on all aspect of performance, providing benchmark services to entire Mumbai,

Thane, and Raigad districts. Technosoft was rewarded in 2011 as the first and only Gold Certified Partner of Xerox India.

> You can see here the manner in which Technosoft ensured that investments in infrastructure followed the growth and stability of the business. Putting in infrastructure ahead of time can lead to financial crunches in day-to-day operations.

Mitesh, the social activist

Mitesh's life would take yet another turn when he came into contact with social activists of the Maharashtra Navnirman Sena (MNS), the political party started by Raj Thackeray. It happened one day that his friends from the MNS party were in a quandary because they had yet to finalise the cover of notebooks that were to be distributed by the MNS to needy school children. Senior party leaders were to inspect the book cover design early next day. Mitesh, the ever willing, offered to help and commenced designing the book cover using Coral Draw. He managed to complete the design in the early hours of the morning and take a couple of printouts, which he took to his friend's house at 2 a.m. in the morning of the day senior party leaders were to be shown the cover design. Mitesh in his imitable style had come up with an effort that received high praise from the MNS leaders.

He was later asked to conduct an eye camp for needy people. This was bread and butter to Mitesh who ran a most successful camp where over 400 people had their eyes checked and attend too. Impressed by his zeal and organising capabilities, the MNS leaders asked him to formally join the MNS and to take on the responsibility of managing the Cable Union. This is a vertical in the MNS, as Mitesh would put it, and a crucial wing of the MNS's activities. He is currently the vice president for the MNS Cable Unions across Maharashtra. Mitesh now spends time in the mornings and evenings on the Union activities and the afternoons at Technosoft. Gradually Dhanpal's sons are being trained to run the operations independently.

This then is the amazing transformation of Mitesh Dave from a service engineer to a product support manager to an outsource service partner to a partner in a firm running Xerox's service operations for the whole of Mumbai and now to a social activist!

Following are his advice to young entrepreneurs and to any young professional:

* Lead a life of independence and self-sufficiency.
* Grab every opportunity that comes your way.
* Be willing to take risks—the bigger the risks, the bigger the gains.
* Be decisive and respect time.
* You will only grow when the people working for you grows.

Mitesh receives an award from Xerox

2. Succeeding from the Brink of Despair—Kulbir's Story

Kulbir's first recollections of the initial days when he opted for the OSAship was how difficult it was for him to resign even though he had made up his mind to take up the outsource opportunity. His manager asked for his resignation letter from service prior to completing the modalities of appointment as an OSA. He thought this strange but went on to write a long resignation letter saying among other things that if the programme failed for any reason, he had the right to be reappointed in Xerox. His manager did not accept this letter and told him that the letter should just be two lines stating his desire to resign from service. Kulbir went outside the office to puff away at a couple of cigarettes, doubts creeping into his mind for the first time, and then he summoned the resolve and went back to the office and wrote out a terse and acceptable resignation letter. From that moment on, he felt relieved and determined to make a great success of his new role. He knew that this was going to be the future business model, besides it would give him the opportunity to be based permanently at Chandigarh, his place of choice.

His search for a job post graduation resulted in a job with Xerox as a service engineer, just one of four graduate engineers in the Punjab Branch. He thought he would be based at Chandigarh, but as it turned out, he was posted at Bhatinda. His job involved hectic travelling, and on a couple of occasions, he witnessed skirmishes with terrorists. After his marriage, he set up home in Patiala, where he had been transferred and equipped it fully with his own funds; he had refused any dowry at the time of his marriage and refused help from his in-laws to equip the house. Kulbir had a mind of his own, as you can see, and as is the case with most successful people had strong ethics and values.

The seeds of entrepreneurship are sown in Kulbir

Living and working in remote locations is excellent learning ground for entrepreneurs. You tend to manage the affairs of the company independently and in a holistic manner and pick up the commercial side of the business, besides the technical aspects. Kulbir had an excellent track record of collecting service contracts and was held as a role model in this regard. He honed the art of selling which would stand him in very good stead when he became an entrepreneur.

In his student days, he would go along with a friend to the friend's father auto repair workshop in Sec 17, the prime commercial sector in Chandigarh. He would help at the auto repair shop and could independently service the carburettor of a scooter or motorcycle. He harboured a deep desire to run a business of his own and have an office in Sec 17. His dream came true when he accepted the OSAship and went on to set up a plush office at Sec 17.

His early days as an OSA were a cakewalk for him. He reluctantly accepted the fax service franchise but quickly saw an opportunity to earn warranty revenue by comprehensive reporting of fax machines sold and installed by sales promotion agents. He also went on a drive of bring-in AMC contracts from the fax machines, post warranty, and soon had a steady additional source of income from these contracts. It was this penchant for revenue generation that enabled him to earn enough to invest in a plot in Mohali.

Kulbir wriggles out of a tight situation

When the revised ASP programme was launched in 2004, Kulbir had to purchase the existing Modi Xerox debt with an investment of Rs 40 lakhs. There were additional investments too, and Kulbir had to sell the plot he had bought to fund the investments required in the business. The early protected days of the OSA programme were over, and the ASP programme would require a different approach to the business. Losses that were being accumulated called for tighter operational controls. Cash flows became a serious problem, and he began to default on payments mainly to the consumables distributor.

His debt reached a staggering Rs 60 lakhs, and the distributor's family members put enormous legal and emotional pressure on him. They were out to have penal action taken against him including having him jailed on criminal charges. The distributor Mr Anil Kapoor, however, put his faith and trust in Kulbir and prevented drastic actions by the other family members. It's rare to see such support in business, and Mr Anil Kapoor was clearly a person of great humanism and values to have supported Kulbir through his dark days.

The filters he set for himself were
* He must own the business and not be a franchisee
* Have the ability to control pricing
* Must have clear value addition from him
* Must have scale and lend itself to retail efforts

Keeping these filters in mind, he has embarked on a set of new initiatives.

When Kulbir looks back at his days as an entrepreneur, he fondly remembers the four-day training programme that had been arranged for the OSA appointees at the RK Khanna Tennis stadium in Delhi. He feels that this was timely instructions on how to run one's own business and a great opportunity to share notes and ideas with the other newly appointed entrepreneurs. Deep down there would be a feeling of gratitude for an opportunity to make a dream come true.

3. Monetising Customer Satisfaction

Customer satisfaction precedes business success, is what the cliché says. For some, customer satisfaction is a necessary evil or the clutch of processes that enable resolution of customer issues. For others, the process of taking feedback and publishing a satisfaction score is an end

Kulbir was determined to turn around the situation he was in ai repay all dues to Mr Anil Kapoor and other creditors. He cut all nee expenses, including smoking, as he felt it cost him not only fo cigarettes he consumed but also for lost time at work. He weeded ou making machines and micromanaged his business. He also took u sales franchise of Xerox products as he felt that the service business will not generate adequate profitability and cash flows.

Kulbir diversified into sales of large format printing machines c and succeeded remarkably well. For three years running, he was v the top five sellers of large format printing systems for HP nationall was invited to attend sales incentive programmes in foreign cou: Gradually and with sheer determination, he paid back all dues interest.

This was a lesson in entrepreneurship in what can be called 'th knocks school' of business. Kulbir today has emerged from this as a well-rounded business man and has the confidence to take c execute more challenging business objectives. Kulbir's experience how important it is to manage finances, be it investments or cash fl

Kulbir approached the initial days of OSAship as just an al work way and perhaps had a traditional 'managers' mindset. The truth dawned upon him that he needed to go into overdrive costs, recover outstanding payments, seek alternate revenue strear maximise returns, and seek additional business lines that will ir profitability and cash inflows. To Kulbir's credit, he got his act tc before it was too late.

At a recent get-together in Dharamshala, I had asked his wife h had coped during the dark period of Kulbir's career as an entrep She told me in a matter of fact way that she had full confiden Kulbir would pull through successfully. I suppose failure was n option for him, and his determination rubbed off on the family.

During a visit to Barcelona for an HP Sales Conference, Kull many successful businessmen, and he concluded that he was tri a business person. He felt that this was possible only when we control the price of his products and services. Without that capabi was just a franchisee of the principles he signed up with. He felt th was to be a true businessman, future business ventures must pass t a set of filters.

in itself. One needs to act only if the scores indicate concern. This is the reactive approach to satisfying customers. For Saravanan, customer satisfaction is an integral part of daily interactions with all customers by all staff members of his organisation. For him, it is the way by which customers feel comfortable doing business with him and the way by which customers are made to feel special and welcome, when dealing with his organisation. The end result is that he runs a self-sustaining and profitable business.

Saravanan shows how to monetise customer satisfaction

Many OSAs were severely burdened by the terms that Xerox offered for purchase of debt when the conversion to the ASP model took place. For Saravanan, this was not a concern at all, as he had converted most of his customers to the Volume Based Service Agreement (VBSA) contract. This was a service arrangement where customers paid in advance for maintenance services that are normally billed and paid for on a monthly basis under the Full Service Maintenance Agreement (FSMA).

> Converting customers to VBSA was a direct result of excellent customer relations and customer satisfaction and an example of monetising customer satisfaction.

When Xerox completed its calculations on the OSAs dues against purchase of debt, it turned out that Xerox had to pay him for un-utilised portions of the service contracts. Saravanan gained the resources needed to fund investments for spares and consumables and had little difficulty in collecting dues.

Good customer relations also enabled him to recommend and secure upgrades to the newer ranges of machines. Knowing his customers and forecasting their needs accurately led him to predict sales for any given period, fairly accurately, and this ensured that he managed his cash flows very well.

> He hardly ever had situations when the stock of machines he took from Xerox or the National Distributors stayed with him beyond a month. With credit of one month for his purchases, he very rarely had any paid stock lying with him. Once again, I attribute this to good customer relations and accurate forecasting. Such accuracy in forecasting can come only with the best of customer relations.

While many ASPs struggled with declining analogue photocopiers and the growth of the less-profitable digital machines, Saravanan managed his business with minimal debt, tight cost management, and cash surpluses through customer advances and proper inventory management. He saw the advantage of selling higher ranges of products and managed sales of a healthy product mix that enabled him to secure larger margins from sales and also meet his sales targets. For me, Saravanan's management of his business is a great example of cashing in on exemplary customer satisfaction.

Saravanan comes from a humble background. His father worked in a transport firm for all of thirty years. This led to certain isolation within his family and social circles, but it instilled in Saravanan a burning desire to do well in life. He was a topper in his school, performed very well in studies at Thiagaraja Polytechnic, and represented the state in caroms! He also secured campus recruitment into Madras Aluminum Company (MALCO) where he worked for a year and a half before joining Xerox at Chennai in December 1989.

Saravanan learns from partners who are senior to him

Saravanan had a very successful career in Xerox. He was selected, through the rigorous Contact Programme, to be the customer service manager at Trichy in Tamil Nadu. It was at Trichy that Saravanan was introduced to the OSA programme and was assigned the responsibility of establishing the OSAship that had been assigned to V Narayanan, a person who was several rungs senior to him in Xerox. Subsequently, he moved to Coimbatore where he supported Ravikanth, his earlier manager, who was the OSA for Coimbatore. Managing partners is always a sensitive task and more so when the partners have been senior to you in the organisation. Saravanan managed these relationships very well as he soaked in all the learning he could on how small business organisations needed to be run and the challenges they would face.

From Narayanan, he learnt the importance of process orientation in managing an operation. He saw the successful migration of the process discipline that was a way of life in Xerox, to the business run by the OSA. He learnt how accounts were to be run to meet the statutory requirements of the tax authorities and the tight control on spares and consumables and customer databases. In both locations, he took responsibility for recruitment of service technicians and their training and development. When he finally got the opportunity to take over the OSAship at Salem, he was very well equipped with what it takes to run a business successfully.

He currently manages a vast territory spread over Salem, Namakkal, Erode, Tirupur, Dharamapuri, and Krishnagiri up to Hosur with engineers based at Salem, Erode, and Tirupur. He has purchased a Maruti Eeco in which two of his staff travelled 200-300 kms every day to meet customers for managing collections and sales of consumables. In addition to his Xerox business, he is a value-adding reseller for laptops and desktops and allied hardware for networking.

Being thrifty by nature, Saravanan made investments in gold and real estate from a very early stage of his working career, and this has added considerably to his net worth and his ability to take loans from banks. He follows a simple formula when going for bank loans against real estate assets. He restricts loans to 25 per cent of the asset value he holds. The VBSA contracts he has also gives him steady income from service revenue.

Saravanan moves ahead in social standing

Over the years, he has added to his educational qualifications with an MBA in Marketing from National Institute of Management, Ahmedabad, and a doctorate in Occult Studies also from the same institute. He now uses this unusual skill as a pastime within his family and friends. Living close to his parents has been a great source of satisfaction to both him and his parents.

Now, as a successful businessman, he has changed the status and fortunes of his family for the good many fold. Saravanan also used the OSA business to provide a livelihood for his brother and four other family members, whom he trained meticulously to be good service engineers and to deal with customers exactly the way he himself would. It is a credit to his grooming and development of these individuals that his brother now has a job with Xerox as a specialist engineer and three of the other four family members have taken up lucrative assignments in Dubai and in India.

He is an active member of the Lions club and served as its president and secretary and was associated with several projects to assist the needy.

Following is the advice that Saravanan has for budding young professionals and entrepreneurs:

* Have a burning desire to achieve the goals you set for yourself.
* You become what you aspire to be, so aim high.
* Build customers relations with a genuine desire to serve them with your heart and soul.
* Build your resources from the beginning through small drops that eventually make an ocean.
* In times of crisis, think positively, and the result will turn out positive.
* Good thoughts, good deeds, good feelings, and good vibrations always give good and great results.

2. Succeeding on the Plank of Values and Principles

Prashant with team members

Talk to Prashant for any length of time and you will not fail to observe that he lives his life and runs his business on the basis of strongly held values and principles. These include being fair and transparent with his employees, a genuine desire to be of service to his customers, and being trustworthy and scrupulously correct in his dealing with all constituencies of his business. These values and principles enabled him to forge long-standing relationships with customers, partners, and principals alike.

Prashant never set out to be an entrepreneur, and like many of his colleagues, he harboured the desire to be a successful service manager. The day he became a customer service manager in Xerox was one of pride and immense satisfaction for him. The unfolding events in Xerox, though, made him realise that outsourcing was the business model of the future, and after a lot of deliberation, he opted to be an OSA and there has been no looking back for him since then.

Prashant had choices a plenty when he completed his diploma in Electrical Engineering in 1993. He got jobs in Bajaj Tempo and Essar Steel through campus recruitment. However, he wanted a field job and applied to and was selected by both HCL and Xerox. He eventually selected Xerox as he was enamoured by the Yezdi motorcycle the job offered and also because of the known faces in Xerox.

In the years to come, when an opening emerged for a branch product sales manager's position in Gujarat, he applied for the same but didn't get the position. He was instead offered the role of a senior territory manager, which he declined. He decided that his career was best served in service management, and he saw a clear career path for himself. He became a Work Group Coordinator for an SMWG team, and subsequently, after assessment at a Contact Centre, he was selected as a customer service manager at Saurastra.

Prashant accepts the validity of service outsourcing

Around this time, the service outsource movement had commenced in Xerox. Prashant could see the organisation growing leaner and flatter and career growth options within the organisation shrinking. He was moved to Surat and was closely involved in the transition of Surat and Vapi to outsource locations.

The outsource model was gradually evolving from a pure labour model to labour plus spares, and Prashant could see that ultimately the model would be an authorised service provider model with full end-to-end responsibility, something that he desired. In many ways, his tenure at Surat had transformed him and gave him a different perspective of his career. He could see and appreciate the changes that the organisation had initiated, and he not only accepted the new business model but also saw in it a future for himself as an outsource partner. He was confident and strongly desirous of being an OSA and building a business of his own.

The opportunity came in tragic circumstances, when the OSA in Ahmedabad, one of the pioneers in this movement, Sajeed Ajmere died in a car accident. Prashant was selected as an OSA for Ahmedabad in 2002 at the age of thirty, a major turning point in his life.

Having a shrewd head for business, Prashant understood that the pure labour model he was operating wasn't lucrative enough and he needed to add revenue streams and sought the distribution of consumables, paper, and the sale of equipment from Xerox. These were not willingly offered to OSAs at that time by Xerox to avoid conflicts with the existing distribution networks. The distributors of all these products, however, saw the strength of the OSAs connect into organisations and willingly offered them products for sale on a commission basis.

In 2003, a year into OSAship, Prashant set up a branch office at Surat and took on as a partner an ex-Xerox colleague, Sanjay Bishnoi, for sales and service of Wipro GE Ultra sound and X-Ray machines. This early foray into new business opportunities was indicative of the business acumen at work in Prashant.

In 2005, major changes in relationships and transformations were taking place within Xerox. Godrej was appointed as the authorised service provider for some locations across the country including Gujarat, and the OSAs of Gujarat were attached to Godrej. At the same time, the disastrous flooding in Surat in 2006 damaged and destroyed his office including all the office equipment and machines in stock.

Sanjay decided to leave the partnership and went back to the corporate world. Prashant took a calculated decision to wind up the Surat operations and concentrate his efforts at Ahmedabad. The intervention of Godrej seemed to close the ASP options for him and presented an uncertain future; however, he felt that Godrej would eventually exit the business and the ASP model would open up for him. He saw this model as the only sustainable model for growth and profitability.

In those grim days when the future was grey and uncertain, many job offers came his way. By now, however, the entrepreneurial flame was burning brightly within him, and he stood steadfast with his decision to build a business of his own. This is the resilience needed for success when one ventures into entrepreneurship.

Prashant expands his business.

He saw a clear gap in the Xerox sales coverage in Gujarat in the government and education segments. The existing sales partners were concentrating on the corporate, SME, and graphic arts segments and losing out to HCL and other companies in the other segments. Prashant made a formal presentation to the Xerox sales team and convinced them to let him sell products in these defined segments without infringing on the territories or accounts of the existing sales partners. In March 2005, Xerox agreed to his proposal, and in fifteen days, he had made sales of over Rs 11 lakhs and since then has been meeting sales targets year on year.

Later in the year, he secured the selling rights for HCL's AVSI solutions, and Prashant was well on his way again. He added to the portfolio the service support for 3M's large medical electronics installations which was a boost to his bottom line. When he reflects on those difficult days, Prashant quotes the famous saying, 'When the Lord closes the door, someone somewhere opens a window'.

To grow the sales business, Prashant took on board Ashutosh Vaishnav, a former sales champion of Xerox, as a partner—a partnership that has remained healthy and thriving to this day. Prashant attributes this to transparency and trust between the two of them and clear understanding on remuneration and profit sharing. That the two operate on the same wave length and on shared values is a strong enabler for the continued success of the partnership. Ashutosh concentrates on sales, while Prashant concentrates on managing and growing the service business.

Once again we see that the seeds for successful partnerships lie in transparency and trust and a clear agreement on the roles and responsibilities of each partner. Also important is clarity on the manner in which profits are distributed.

In 2007, Godrej exited the business as Prashant had foreseen, opening the way for the four OSAs of Gujarat to unite as one entity and take over from Godrej. This they did and transferred all their existing Xerox service business into the new entity. They also opened a twenty-seater call centre for Tata Teleservices. However, it was not long before this partnership fractured.

Predictably, the root causes for the break up were lack of trust and transparency and differing views on how the business should be run. One of the unfortunate features of the OSA programme has been the inability of the partners to come together and function as a single entity over a long period of time. This has prevented acceleration in their growth. This is where I believe Xerox programme managers should have played a supportive role.

Business suffered, and Xerox was deeply concerned on the ability of the united company to function effectively. Prashant was able to convince Xerox on transferring the machines in field in Ahmedabad to his company on the ASP terms being offered at that time, with the assurance that the transition would take place smoothly without any loss of revenue or customer satisfaction. The transition took place most smoothly in thirty days, and the business has been flourishing since then.

Prashant creates an environment in his company that attracts and retains talent

Prashant ran his company with policies and practices normally seen in larger companies. He introduced a compensation plan for his employees that had a fixed and variable component. In fact, he gradually introduced this remuneration pattern and secured the acceptance of his employees. Through this strategy, he has ensured that his employees have a stake in the company's success and he in turn can direct team effort based on the priorities of the year, through the performance parameters he sets for the variable component. Clearly, this requires accurate and simple measurement systems and transparency and trust within the team. Every year, Prashant sets aside 50 per cent of the company's profits to fund salary increases. This was a very neat way of ensuring participation by the employees in the profitability of the company.

It is no wonder that Prashant has a high-retention rate for his strong team of forty-two members and attracts and recruits staff from larger and more established companies. Employee initiatives include training and development, and Prashant proudly says that he has a former machine operator who now heads the supplies business and former courier boys who are now successful salesmen. Prashant runs a grand slam completion much like Xerox, and for the last few years, he has been sending the top three or four employees to holiday destination around the world.

Prashant makes no bones about micromanaging his business as he feels this is essential for success. It's for this reason that he doesn't seek to enter into too many different business lines. He prefers to stay concentrated in a few carefully chosen businesses and grow organically within each of them. He makes investment decisions in his business such that for every 33 paisa spend on salaries, he expects gross profit of Rs 1, and for all investment made, he expects a payback in not more than eighteen months.

Clarity of thought and an uncluttered approach to business are what stick out when you analyse his business. Simple but clear expectations on any investment, a pro employee approach, and micromanagement are the principles on which he runs his business. This is an excellent model for any budding entrepreneur.

Following are Prashant's advice to young entrepreneurs:
* Do whatever you endeavour correctly the first time, and don't adopt short cuts
* Manage your funds, cash flows, and receivables
* Be genuinely concerned about your customers and employees, and ensure your team also shows the same concern for customers.
* Stay steadfast to your values and principles, and select team members and partners who share these values

Prashant with his team

Ashutosh Vaishnav wins a Xerox award

5. Building a Life of Value

Hari inaugurating Jatinder's office

I associate Amritsar very much with Jatinder and his younger brother Harpreet ever since my first visit to inaugurate his office in June 1998, along with a team from Modi Xerox. Jatinder was the inspiration behind

71

a get-together with some of the OSAs in April 2013, which brought me back in touch with these very fine businessmen.

As we closed the visit, Jatinder suggested we go for an early morning visit to the Golden Temple. He patiently explained the day-long rituals at the temple and offered to pick me up at 3.30 a.m. to reach the Golden Temple at 4 a.m.! I agreed, and it was a wonderful experience. Over the past year and a half, Jatinder has made this a regular practice, a glorious start for him each day at the crack of dawn, which he believes is possible only through the divine grace of God.

A humble beginning and early struggles

Jatinder comes from a humble background. His grandmother became a widow at the age of seventeen and struggled to bring up her two sons, his father and uncle. His father served for a while in the Home Guards before he took up a clerical position in the Ministry of Irrigation. His mother was a school teacher.

Jatinder's father was very keen that he studied civil engineering and become an engineer in the Ministry of Irrigation. He would very often take him to see the construction activity at irrigation sites and to meet the senior divisional officer, a civil engineer and who the father hoped would be a role model for his son. But Jatinder had other interests and was keen on being an electronics engineer and eventually convinced his father that this was the better career for him. He was unable to clear the entrance exams for engineering colleges in Punjab but with his father's support secured admission in an engineering college in Nasik.

He completed his engineering education and secured a job through campus recruitment at Siemens but wanted to live and work in Punjab, so he declined the offer and returned to Amritsar to look for a job.

Times were tough and jobs hard to come by, as he went knocking on door to door facing demoralizing rejections everywhere. Eventually, he took up a sales job with Mr Nagpal's company, Global Business Solutions, a sales partner of Modi Xerox at Amritsar. He did a very good job selling entry-level inkjet printers, and this served as an excellent foundation for his career as an entrepreneur. His heart, however, was on a technical job, and he would accompany Jagmohan who was then a customer service engineer with Modi Xerox, based at Jammu. Jagmohan would tell him about the technical aspects of the machines he was attending and also trained him to take service calls. Jagmohan then recommended that he be recruited as a service engineer in Modi Xerox, and after the due processes of recruitment, he finally had a job more to his liking and aptitude in 1995 and was posted at Jalandhar. It is only fitting that Jagmohan who helped Jatinder find a foothold in life is himself now a successful entrepreneur at Dharamshala.

Harpreet had an equally difficult start to his career. He had to drop out of college, as the remnants of terrorist activity in the state were still on and the atmosphere in the college was not conducive to learning. He joined his uncle's stationary shop as a helper on pocket money of Rs 300 per month. His tasks among others included cleaning the shop and making daily visit to Ludhiana to pick up supplies from a larger stationary shop run by other family members. When Jatinder returned to Amritsar on transfer from Jalandhar, he helped Harpreet get a job in a sister company of Global Business Systems as a salesman for the Cease Fire range of products. This helped hone his selling skills. He then enrolled for the GNIIT course, through evening classes, and this not only gave him the confidence to make effective sales presentations but taught him the IT skills that he would use as Jatinder expanded his business operations.

Jatinder seizes the opportunity to build a business of his own

When the OSAship was offered to him, Jatinder saw it as a wonderful opportunity to build a business of his own in Amritsar. He did not have the financial resources to run a business, a dream he nurtured; besides, his father had grave misgivings on his leaving a settled job. He clearly told him that the decision was solely his and that he wouldn't be in a position to help financially in any way. Moreover, his marriage had been fixed for later that year and financial instability would do no good to his marriage plans.

It was with a great deal of uncertainty and anxiety that Jatinder accepted the OSAship, banking on the Rs 1.50 lakhs loan that Modi Xerox offered to him along with staggered payment terms for the royalty payment he had to make to takeover the SSMA machines from Modi Xerox. Wisely, Harpreet joined him and focused on service contract collections. When the initial payments to Modi Xerox could be made out of the revenue generated from the business, Jatinder developed the confidence that he could run the business and manage the cash flows. Harpreet continued to focus on the sales and revenue generation side of the business as he preferred that to the technical side of the business.

> Service outsourcing has such heart-warming opportunities for the employees of a company. When a company offers support to its employees to take up such entrepreneurial opportunities and nurses them through the initial difficult phases, they create a very strong and loyal base of service partners. Many companies ignore this principle and create instead an atmosphere of distrust.

Jatinder knew that if he had to grow his business, he needed to think beyond purely service outsourcing. In 2006, Xerox offered him the sales franchise of their products, and this not only grew revenue but strengthened the service business through increased machine population. He rightfully saw himself not just as a franchisee of Xerox but as a businessman. He took on additional lines of business with varying degrees of success. He learnt quickly that he cannot afford to defocus on the primary line of the Xerox sales and service business. He also decided not to spread his efforts too thinly and sought logical extension to the Xerox line of business. This truth struck him after a failed business partnership with a group of OSAs who set up a company in Delhi called Puntech Solutions.

> A problem that Jatinder has been facing all through his tenure as an entrepreneur is his inability to provide time and attention to new business lines. The inability of the OSAs of Punjab to establish a sustainable partnership and jointly grow their business is hampering the implementation of several business ideas he has. Building partnership is one of the planks for business growth. The OSAs seem to have fallen into the trap of being too independent in the way they run their business and too wedded to the thought processes that enabled them to stabilise their fledgling businesses and run them successfully. Forging partnerships as we saw earlier requires a clear understanding of roles and responsibilities, trust and transparency, and a clear understanding of remuneration patterns and the manner in which profits will be shared. Trust between these colleagues is a big stumbling block as I see it. Perhaps Jatinder could look for partners outside the OSA community and set up a platform for growth. Here again facilitation by Xerox programme managers would have helped.

He found a gap in the Xerox product portfolio at the lower end and entered into an agreement with Sharp for sales and service of a range of printers below 20 cpm. For products above 20 cpm, he continued to offer the Xerox range. This clear demarcation of product ranges helped ensure that he gave adequate focus and attention to both principals. In addition, he started training classes to impart IT skills at schools and through this effort to sell IT hardware and services also. Harpreet created a course that enables school teachers to appreciate the power of the Internet by introducing them to good informative websites and video-based learning modules, and he also created a library of over 500 web-based learning lessons for the school teachers to refer to and use.

Now role models in their family and social circles

The people of Punjab are known for their hard working and entrepreneurial nature. Jatinder and Harpreet were no exceptions, and through dint of hard work and application, they have made a success of the entrepreneurial venture they had embarked on over a decade ago, with so much uncertainty.

Today, they have the net worth and financial resources that would only have been a distant dream for their parents and grandparents. They have built a large house, each half being a mirror image of the other for each of the brothers. This was a great desire of their father, and the sons made it happen in the lifetime of their parents. Their father was able to see this dream come true before his demise in 2008. Both the brothers are now valued members of their extended family, who turn to them to offer inspiration and career counselling to their children!

Jatinder's mantra for budding entrepreneurs is
* Focus, concentrate, and micromanage all you do
* Don't scatter your efforts too widely
* Don't let the 'core' areas of your business suffer

Like all good entrepreneurs, Jatinder has the passion and vision that drives him. He now wishes to establish a finishing school for graduate engineers and diploma holders to make them ready for the real world and better equipped to secure jobs of their choice. It is an ambitious project, but given his dedication and application and the mantras that he swears by, I am sure he will create an institution he can be proud of; forging effective partnerships would help establish his dream.

Harpreet and Jatinder

6. Succeeding in the Alternate Career Option.

Jagmohan was one of the first to take up the OSAship in the remote locations, a natural choice for service outsourcing. He chose the quaint town of Dharamshala, District Kangra (H.P.), way back in April 1999, and today, fourteen years on, he is a standing example of the efficacy of the alternate career option.

Jagmohan was born in Chandigarh where he spent the initial years of his life before leaving home, at the age of eleven, to join the Sainik School at Sujanpur Tira, District Hamirpur (HP). Thereafter, he went on to complete B. Tech (Electrical) from Regional Engineering College, Hamirpur (HP). Then, like so many graduates, he struggled to find a job, letting a couple of small companies pass as he didn't want to join them. He took on a tuition assignment with a fifth standard student and earned Rs 750 per month, just enough to cover his routine expenses. Fortuitously, his father, who was working in a government organisation in Chandigarh, met a Xerox Sales Manager and asked him if there was an opening for his son. The sales manager, Mr Lalit Mathur, forwarded Jagmohan's resume to the customer service manager, and after the due process of selection, he was recruited as a service engineer, a job he accepted with a great deal of pride.

Initially posted at Jammu and subsequently at Pathankot, Jagmohan had the typically hard and taxing life of a service engineer based in a remote location. He had to cover several far flung districts of Himachal Pradesh, Jammu, and Punjab, and invariably, his day would start at 5.30 a.m. and close after 10 p.m. with long and strenuous hours of scooter riding. This daily grind also required him to build the best of relations with his customers and to handle all related aspects of his job, including service contract collections, follow-up of sales leads, and securing repeat sales. Service engineers of remote locations learn to be all-rounders and learn to be both self-sufficient and self-reliant. They learn to manage very much on their own with little support from their Regional offices.

Jagmohan accepts OSAship as the option that will keep him in Dharamshala

It was late in 1998 that Jagmohan was first approached by his managers with the offer of the OSAship. Over the years, he had little time to think of his career or the directions the company was taking or to seek opportunities for growth; his was the life of a hard working, honest service engineer. Intuitively, he knew that outsourcing seemed to be the way of the future. Besides, as he said, the running cost of maintaining remote and scattered territories was too high for the company in the existing business model.

He saw just a few options before him, to take up the OSAship or seek a transfer to another location or take up a specialist role in the emerging fields of colour copiers or high-end printing systems and relocate to a metro. He chose what his heart told him and that was to take up the OSAship at Dharamshala and remain within the Kangra District, the place his family belonged to.

He had made up his mind that this was the place he would like to live and earn a living for the rest of his life. While his father readily accepted the new life that Jagmohan was embarking on, his mother needed loads of convincing before she too gave him her blessings.

When the terms of the OSAship were being finalised, Jagmohan had only Rs 696 in his bank account. The programme managers ensured that he received the SSMA contract transfers of Rs 2.84 lakhs from Xerox immediately by demand draft and allowed him to pay the royalty payments of Rs 2.64 lakhs in four equal instalments. This was the support he badly needed and the enabler to kick-start his operations. His father supported him with a further Rs 50,000, a loan still lying in his books, as he has sadly passed away.

Support came from several quarters. Dr Sudharshan Chakra and Mr Vijay Mahajan considered him an honest and hard working youngster and a role model for the youngsters of Dharamshala and offered him a room in premises owned by the Red Cross free of cost, for his office. He availed of this kind gesture for two years before he moved into an office of his own. His father helped set up the accounting systems, and his wife Meena ran the office and accounts.

With just 132 machines and two technicians, this would be probably one of the smallest service outsource operations in the country. Parsimonious operations and judicious use of the surpluses generated over the first few years of operations ensured the continued viability of the operations.

The offer of Xerox sales dealership in the year 2000 also helped build viability. In later years, the lower service revenues both from contract collections and consumables sales were offset by reducing running costs and maintaining profitability to reasonable levels.

That operations of this relatively small scale could be managed profitably over such a long period of time speak for the efficient management by Jagmohan and the efficacy as we said of the alternate career option.

Jagmohan succeeds in leading a balanced life

When Jagmohan looks back over the years, he has much to be proud of and the satisfaction of leading a balanced life with quality time for the family and social obligations. He invested in a plot of land and constructed, over a period of time, a beautiful three-storied house with a vegetable garden that produces most of the household's need for vegetables. His wife, Meena, is a picture of cheerfulness, and whatever reservations she may have had in those fateful early days of OSAship in 1999 are long gone and forgotten. Jagmohan's sons Purvansh and Divyansh are still in school and have a bright future to look forward to.

Jagmohan was never the person to seek his fortunes in the corporate rat race. Just as the OSAship had offered to him and many others an alternate way of life, Jagmohan had chosen an alternate lifestyle: balancing work and life, living and working in a place of his choice, and leading a life relatively free of the mad rush and tensions of today's world. As I spent time with him talking of his experiences and life choices, I could see that Jagmohan had made the right choices for himself and his family, touch wood.

Jagmohan's advice to budding entrepreneurs is simple: never cheat and never tell lies, manage your time well, and always keep to your time commitments to customers and business partners.

7. Charting His Own Path

Ramchandran

Like many stalwarts, Ram had put in decades of service for his organisation, working with dedication and result-oriented, but inevitably, the time would come for him to give way to younger aspirants and to chart a path of his own. This is what Ram has successfully accomplished after a career spanning two long decades.

Ram spent most of his younger days, in fact most of his working life in Mumbai. He did his schooling from Holy Family High School, a Jesuit school that shaped his value system and principles and prepared him to lead a disciplined and ethical life. He went on to complete a four-year course in Electrical and Electronics Engineering from VJTI Matunga before he joined DCM Data Product as a service engineer for their computer systems and 80-column dot matrix printers, and then joining Xerox at the Cuffe Parade office.

Ram joined Xerox as a Regional trainer in 1985 and thereafter moved upwards quickly to positions of customer service manager, senior customer service manager, and then branch service manager, before leaving Xerox in 1992 to take up an assignment as general manager of a company dealing with Panasonic products in Nigeria. He returned three years later in 1995 as his family wanted to relocate back to India and Ram too was of the opinion that an extended stay in Nigeria was not helping him grow or develop professionally.

On his return from Nigeria, within just a week, he received a call from RICOH, where several ex-Xerox employees had moved, to take up the position of branch service manager, and an appointment letter was given to him while he was asked to wait in the office after the interview. RICOH didn't want him to reach out to Xerox and was pre-empting any efforts by him to join Xerox. In turn, Xerox called him over and promptly offered him the position of Regional Service Manager to take over from another stalwart KG Pillai, who was leaving to join Motorola as the National Service Head. Ram's offer letter was given to him on the spot by Xerox. When you are in the prime of your career, companies fall over each other in the attempt to recruit you. Sadly, in the later days of your career, the same enthusiasm to recruit you is rarely shown.

Ram had very little time to take over from KG Pillai and had to hit the ground running. He was in charge of the service operations of a large territory comprising Maharashtra, Gujarat, Bhopal, and Goa. Mumbai itself had five districts. He managed a talented team which included Surendran, Nadu More, Bhargav Mistry, Ravi Kartha, Nitin Jagtap, Naren Raykar, and many more who went on to do very well in their careers both inside Xerox and also in large corporations outside. Managing a talented group and getting the best out of them requires a special skill, which Ram displayed in full measure.

Under Ram's leadership, the Western Region was a front-runner for all the performance awards with a healthy representation in all the high-profile annual grand slam recognition events run by Xerox. In 1997, Region West stood *number one* in the country in the annual CSMS, and he decided to take the entire team of Region West including work controllers, engineers, and others to Bangkok for four days, with the price money which was substantial. This in itself was a record.

His teams also performed very creditably and often led the rest of the country on several initiatives such as the 'COR' or the material yield improvement programme, the refurbishing programme, the annuity improvement programme, and so on. He also took the lead in several major initiatives, such as the launch of the SMWG Programme, the Centralized Work Control facility at Vikhroli, and also in the outsourcing initiatives. Ram, like many stalwarts of the service industry, was result-oriented and went all out to achieve the objectives set for his team in every endeavour. Yet he always looked for improvements and took the lead to go down on a discovery mission to the Southern Region along with one of his CSMs to observe the data and reporting discipline maintained in that region. It is with justifiable pride that Ram recollects his days as the service head of the Western Region and carries a strong feeling of accomplishment.

> As the head of the Western Region, Ram had a crucial role in rolling out the Service Outsource Programme and in selecting and grooming the early adopters of the programme.

The role a regional leader plays in the successful implementation of programmes is immensely important and can make or break initiatives. That so many team members, including senior managers, opted for it is a tribute to his successful roll-out of the programme. Ram also had a firsthand view of what was going well with the programme and the pain points for the OSA partners. The annual kick off meets he used to conduct for the OSA partners were eagerly awaited and were rewarding for the partners. He was quick to spot if an OSA was unduly concentrating on the revenue and profitability aspects of the business and not taking a holistic view including customer satisfaction and loyalty.

He encouraged partners to diversify into non competing areas when Xerox had no objection to the same as he felt this was imperative for growth and profitability improvement. The OSAs of Gujarat and Pune were particularly successful in diversifying their businesses.

In 2005, when Godrej was appointed by Xerox as the National Service Provider, Ram seriously considered making a bid to run Mumbai as an ASP. The investments required and the investments needed to purchase the debt were worrying elements. Also he needed to forge partnerships with others who would be the financers and he was worried at his likely positioning in such a set-up.

At times like these, the power and prestige of your current position and your inability to let go of it can be the single biggest stumbling block to moving ahead decisively. The terms of engagement in the corporate world and those in an entrepreneurial venture are different when one is a senior manager, and one needs to recognise and reconcile to this.

The missed opportunity, however, didn't prove too costly for Ram as Godrej pulled out of the operations in 2006 and the opportunity presented itself again. Ram discussed with Dhanpal Parikh of Elegant Stationers to consider making the investment of approximately Rs 1.5 crore to bid for being the ASP for Mumbai. He made a detailed investment plan and an ROI calculation for the project. He also forged a partnership between Elegant Stationers and Mitesh Dave and Mansingh Mohite, both of whom ran service outsource operations in Mumbai and were earlier attached to Godrej. Ram had some years ago induced Dhanpal Parikh, who was then only a paper supplies partner of Xerox to take up the distribution of photocopier consumables. He had agreed to this, and this has now become a very lucrative business line for Elegant Stationers.

> This is an excellent example of guiding and supporting the formation of an alliance and the integration of a financial partner. This supportive approach needed to be put in place by Xerox across the country.

Ram left Xerox and joined the partnership, but he did not stay in this partnership beyond eight months as he was not entitled to a share of the profits, not having invested any money in the company and was technically just an employee.

On leaving Xerox, he had prudently requested and received the ASPship of Nasik. The earlier ASP, Ganesh Kavle, had exited the business to set up a third party operation of his own and an interim arrangement was on at Nasik. Ram ran the Nasik office through an employee and through weekend visits while he was with Technosoft. Once he exited the Mumbai partnership, he concentrated his attention on a full-time basis on the Nasik venture.

The Nasik operation is relatively small and has staff strength of just seven. Returns from the business are nominal, but as Ram say, his aim is not to be making large sums of money but to stay engaged and be active.

Nevertheless, he has hit upon the right engagement plan where he is putting efforts into securing large-size sales deals from large companies. Recent successes at the India Security Press and HAL have brought him significant sales incentives and healthy and recurring after-sales revenues. Ram has fashioned for himself a path of his own and has successfully extended his active career after his tenure at Xerox came to an end.

Ram's advice to budding entrepreneurs is
* Keep expenses to a bare minimum (no fancy offices).
* Domain knowledge of your business is essential as it cannot be delegated.
* Forge partnerships with care; there must be a clear understanding of what each partner brings to the table and clear agreements on the financial arrangements and profit sharing.
* Maintain a diversified business portfolio.

C. The Pains of Dropping Out

That some should drop out of a programme of this nature is inevitable; I selected for this analysis two early adopters, who I felt were not likely to drop out. **Sandeep** ran one of the pilots for the service outsource programme and for long was the 'poster' boy of the programme, since he was based in Delhi.

Sandeep enjoyed the initial activities of designing and setting up the office and the work practices and processes. Also his father, who had just retired, took an active part in running the admin and accounts operations, and Sandeep may have seen this as a spin-off benefit of the outsource option.

When his father passed away, Sandeep started reassessing his options and what he wanted to achieve in his professional career. When the revenue sharing model was introduced and his profitability dipped, the scales decisively tilted in favour of his returning to the corporate world. He is doing well for himself now and has reason to feel proud and satisfied with his achievements. Perhaps the entrepreneurial instinct was not strong within him.

Dinesh's story is one of breaking away on account of profitability pressures and the trust deficit that was building up in his relations with Xerox. His return to the corporate world was never fully satisfying but in some ways helped him lay the foundation for a return to entrepreneurship. I refer to this as reigniting the smouldering embers of entrepreneurship.

1. Taking the Learning Back to the Corporate World

Sandeep with Rita Garcia

Sandeep Singhal joined Xerox in 1989 at the age of twenty-one, after completing a post diploma in Electrical Engineering from the YMCA Institute of Engineering in Faridabad. With his first salary, a stipend of Rs 1,300, he bought a Sanyo Walkman, a prized possession that he still has with him. He always dreamt of being a service manager in Xerox, and this drove his career choices in later years.

Sandeep was selected to run a pilot outsource programme, the routine maintenance operations, at Delhi, the forerunner of the eventual service outsource programme at Modi Xerox. He was one of two selected for the pilot, the other being Ramki at Chennai. For Ramki, it was a God-sent opportunity, and he grasped it with both hands and went on to become a successful entrepreneur. Sandeep took a u-turn after a good and promising start and decided to get back to the corporate world. There are lessons to be learnt from Sandeep's career choices, and it is well worth exploring them.

At the age of 45 in May 2013, when Sandeep talked of his career highlights, he refers to his 3½ years as an OSA as the golden period in his life. A time of great learning for him, and I dare say a refreshing freedom to plan and act as he thought fit. Sandeep strikes me as a person with strong values and an independent streak which may not have always pleased his service managers. This may very well have been one of the reasons for him being chosen to run the pilot outsource programme. His uncle, Vinod Gupta, a senior manager at Modi Xerox also advised him that an entrepreneurial role would be the best for him. (Vinod and Brij Chandiramani went on to start a successful and highly rated training and leadership development institution of their own.)

Was Sandeep the right choice for an OSA?

The decision of the service managers to get Sandeep to opt for the service outsource programme may well have been right, as Sandeep has the skills and qualities to be a successful entrepreneur. His father, who had recently retired, was also keen on his taking up this new role and stepped in to offer help in running the back office activities. However the lingering doubt in Sandeep's mind was that he had little chance to progress as a service manager and felt that the outsource option was being offered as an honourable option for him.

It was not surprising, therefore, that when push came to shove, he opted to get back into the corporate world. When you opt to be an entrepreneur, it needs to be driven by the desire to set up and successfully run an operation of your own and to seize a business opportunity and turn it into reality. When the prime mover is an honourable alternative worth a shot, the experiment may well be short-lived.

> Entrepreneurship calls for a high degree of resolve to take the rough with the smooth and the staying power to live through tough times. Sandeep's choice as an OSA in hindsight is very questionable. Choice of partners is a very crucial element of an outsource programme, and the people selected as partners must display a strong desire to take the entrepreneurial route. He also needs to display the requisite commercial acumen, leadership qualities, and the drive to make a success of the business he is entering into.

Sandeep threw himself into the new role, and as I said earlier, he enjoyed the freedom it offered to him. He enjoyed the effort needed to build his office and operations from scratch, including the design and layout of the office, the tool kit design and procurement, setting up of the office procedures and systems, and planning the service operations based on the machine spread and usage pattern. His father was a great help in streamlining the accounts and other office procedures.

Being a pioneer and that to at the HQ of the company, he had many occasions to be in the limelight through frequent visits and reviews by senior managers and showcase visits from Xerox managers from the US and UK. Everyone who saw and had occasion to review his operations were unanimous that his was a very well-run operation. Sandeep also carried a deep faith that the organisation would support him at all times.

The seeds of doubt are planted in Sandeep's mind

So when did the disillusion come about? Many events that followed one after the other had a cumulative impact on Sandeep's decision to head back to the corporate world. His father passed away in 2002 making him relook the purpose and direction of his life. A brief stint of a year or so as a service franchise of Whirlpool left him discontented as he found it difficult to bring in changes and the improvements that he felt necessary. They were not open to change as he would say. The Xerox service outsource programme was undergoing several changes, and he experienced shrinking earnings. He was uncertain of opportunities to expand his operations and was disinclined to take up product sales. Opportunities to get back into the corporate world were alluring and beckoning, and it was not long before he resigned as an OSA and took up a job once more.

Sandeep wins his spurs in the corporate world

He was a firm believer in destiny and felt that he was being guided along a path that would make his dream of being a service manager true. He first joined Gestetner and then returned to Xerox as a Regional Service Manager in the Printing Systems Division. It was everything he wanted and desired, that is, being a service manager at Xerox and in a field where there was a lot for him to learn. He felt the environment at Xerox a bit distant and cold, and when the opportunity came his way, he moved to Canon as the National Service Head for the Printing Systems Products. He has a very fulfilling role and believes more than ever that his life has evolved in the most appropriate way for him. He is currently at the pinnacle of his career.

His key learning from the entrepreneurship which helped him in the corporate world, he says, are financial planning and prudence, managing situational setbacks, prudent staffing through rotation of manpower to keep the motivation high, and many more. His stint as an entrepreneur made him a much more rounded manager and this I am sure has lead to his success in the corporate world. When he looks back at his pre-OSA days in the corporate world and the current post-OSA days, he can justifiably feel proud of the progress he has made.

When Sandeep looks ahead at his life, he may ask what next. Is he in the reckoning to take higher responsibilities in his current organisation or in any other? How will he need to equip himself to ensure he doesn't stagnate and lose the drive to perform? I am sure he will grapple successfully with these issues and go on to cap a very rewarding and fulfilling career.

The last thing he told me as we closed our meeting over a cup of coffee was that he still treasures his SMWG Manual and plans to show it to his son!

With Vic Norman and Hari

2. Igniting the Smouldering Embers of Entrepreneurship

Dinesh at his office

Dinesh Nandwani's story is the classical tussle between the security of the corporate world and venturing out into the uncertainty of the entrepreneurial world. In the end, the pull of the entrepreneurial world won and the smouldering embers of entrepreneurship are now ablaze with opportunity and hope.

Dinesh joined Xerox in 1989 as a customer engineer trainee and rose steadily in the hierarchy to being a senior CE, then technical specialist supporting the outsource agents (TS-OS), and then a customer support manager (CSM). He was always seen as a hard-working and dependable manager and was invariably given critical territories to manage, and he generally delivered satisfactory results.

It was while serving as a TS-OS that the seeds of entrepreneurship were sown within him. He witnessed at first hand the efforts of Ajay Bhuttan, the OSA he was supporting, and through discussions with Sandeep Singhal, he knew he could successfully manage operations of this nature. Puneet Gargya, who was then the Regional OSA Programme Manager, also influenced his decision to opt for being an OSA.

It was in May 2000 that Dinesh finally took the plunge and signed up for the OSA programme. He was given the territory of Gurgaon and South Delhi and had a team of twelve tech reps and one work controller. His father who had retired in April 2002 joined him to assist in the HR and administration-related activities and immensely liked the assignment. By 2003, his operations had increased to twenty-five tech reps, and subsequently, when Sandeep had resigned from the OSAship, he took over his territory and managed a large operation of fifty tech reps and three work controllers and 5,500 active machines in field. His area of operations included all the key accounts of Xerox, an indication of how trustworthy Dinesh was considered.

Trouble was around the corner as can be expected. In 2005, Godrej took over as the service partner for the National Capital Region (NCR.) A group of OSAs had been given an opportunity to take this role, but as it involved the purchase of large debt and higher investments in the business, the OSAs didn't opt for it and chose instead to become service partners of Godrej. This brought about a reduction in margins, higher turnaround times for spares, and delays in payments to the service partners, leading to cash flow difficulties. The first payment to Dinesh reached him after a period of three months. Later that year, Dinesh dropped out of the OSA programme.

The entrepreneurial seed had taken root for Dinesh, and he ventured into a direct sales agent (DSA) operation with Tata Indicom along with a partner. This operation would wind up due to disputes between the partners. He also took up a sales distributorship for Dish TV along with a cousin. The Dish TV business got off to a good start with a 250-active dealer base and twenty-five installation teams. However, his father's illness drew him away from day-to-day operations and required his cousin to step up and run the business. Unfortunately, his cousin could not take on this responsibility, and the business was terminated with substantial losses on account of payment defaults by dealers.

> There are lessons a plenty for any budding entrepreneur in this case study, and these include the care and detailing necessary in drawing up partner agreements upfront and the need to allow for fall back options. What each partner brings to the partnership and the ability to contribute is an important consideration.

These setbacks took Dinesh back to the corporate world. He joined HCL and then moved to Aforeserve and then RT Outsourcing (now Intarvo). Luckily, for Dinesh, all these moves only added to his entrepreneurial learning and further prepared him for his eventual return to the world of entrepreneurship. At HCL, he ran a pilot for telesales of World Space connections and also management of the installations.

He was also involved in the setting up of the first 'repair factory' for Nokia mobile phone repairs. It is a far cry from the current world-class facilities that HCL runs but nevertheless gave him valuable exposure that would stand him in good stead later. At Aforeserve, he was involved in the establishment of the franchised service network 'Restore' that had been set up for mobile phone repairs. While the programme itself was far from successful, it once again gave him valuable insights into running outsourced business operations. At RT Outsourcing, he was involved in managing mobile phone repairs and the installation support for migration of Airtel DTH customers to the new satellite services. This would turn out to be the arena that encouraged Dinesh to break out on his own once again.

Dinesh prepared a detailed business plan for undertaking service operations for Airtel's DTH services on a national basis. The project was likely to require an investment of several crores of rupees, so Dinesh secured the support of a financier who had interests in real estate. The aim was to take advantage of the government's plans to introduce Conditional Access Services (CAS) around the middle of 2012. Dinesh secured a National Agreement with Airtel, and offices were established at Delhi, Mumbai, and Kolkata with Chennai to follow. He was given a monthly salary and a profit-sharing plan by the financier. However, delays in launch of the CAS regime made the financier restless, and he pulled out of the business reneging on Dinesh's monthly payouts. It took months of effort for him to successfully wind down the operations that comprised of three offices and a staff of approx forty employees.

Choice of business partners is such a crucial component of large-scale entrepreneurial ventures. It was good that he went for an ambitious project, but he would always have needed the right partners and a team to achieve sustained success. Agreeing on a business plan with the financier, agreeing to clear roles and responsibilities, and a written agreement on the manner in which profits will be shared are essentials in a partner agreement. In this case, I believe that Dinesh was extremely positive about the prospects of the business and badly needed a financier. He ended up being an employee and not a partner. Choice of the partner in any case was questionable.

Undaunted Dinesh went ahead with his entrepreneurial plans and, being convinced of the viability of the DTH business, signed up as an Installation Service Provider with Dish TV with eleven on-roll staff and fifteen off-roll installation crew teams. So good was his operations over the initial months that he was immediately converted into a sales and service partner. He has plans to set up a seventy-five-seat Test and Repair facility for set top boxes and mobile phones and hopes to secure business from Dish TV and other brands in the DTH and mobile phone space. After a long and at times disappointing journey of twists and turns, the smouldering embers of entrepreneurship are well and truly ablaze for Dinesh. It's early days, yet the spirit is strong and the future bright. Dinesh will march along undaunted by setbacks and hopefully will find his place in the sun.

Dinesh's key learning from corporate experience and setbacks in business ventures are mentioned below:

* Agree upfront on roles and responsibilities and boundaries for decision-making when working in partnership
* Periods of setbacks are golden learning opportunities
* There is always a ray of hope in the face of setbacks
* There is entrepreneurship learning even while in corporate assignments.
* Follow systems and processes at every step of life; this will help in achieving goals more quickly and easily.

---

6. BREAKING FREE

When the OSA programme was launched way back in 1998, the intent was to create a partner network that would stand Xerox in very good stead and be an enabler for its continued dominance in the market place. It was always expected that some would drop out or choose to leave the Xerox fold and that some may even need to be terminated as partners. However, it was expected that the core would remain intact for a decade or more and form the nucleus of an enviable partner network.

When we look back, a little over a decade since the launch of the programme, it's sad that far too many of the early adaptors have left the Xerox fold. The benefits of the platform that was so assiduously put together has not resulted in the gains that the company should have reaped.

While the company's strategic direction may have changed sharply, away from the low—and mid-volume machines to the niche high-end printing solutions and colour copiers, the company could have benefitted much more through product sales and service revenue from the products it choose to operate through a partner network.

It's ironic that the OSA network that could have served as the platform for such revenue and profitability growth was not put to full use. This is why I am inclined to say that the benefits that were foreseen at the launch of the programme were not fulfilled for the company while it may have helped achieve individual goals.

A. Erosion of Old Values

A universal assessment by all the OSAs whom I met or spoke to has been the deterioration in the way Xerox evolved over the years. For obvious reasons, those that left the Xerox fold were more vocal, while those still with Xerox were guarded in their comments. This is what they had to say:

* A marked drop in the win-win approach and more intent on meeting Xerox's immediate goals.
* Growing distance from ground realities and low field coverage by Xerox managers.
* Weak policy implementation.

It was always the intent of the programme to gradually move away from the protection of the early years and to require more investments by the partners in an authorised service provider mode of operations. It was also expected that the high level of field support would be tapered down after the initial years. This would pose challenges in monitoring and control of operations and needs structured review and partner engagement processes. Also needed would be a clear agreement on service deliverables.

It was foreseen that the analogue machines which formed the bulk of the service revenue stream for the partners would be reduced and replaced by the less-profitable digital machines. If the partners stayed rooted to the original outsourcing sphere, their revenues and profitability would drop year on year till it became unviable to continue. Concern for partner viability must therefore have been one of the prime considerations of the programme managers. The introduction of the ASP model should also have been done with concern for the financial stability of the partners and the necessary support put in place.

For the long-term survival of the partners, it was necessary for them to diversify, and options were given to them at an early stage to take up consumables sales and subsequently the sale of machines. Taking up non-Xerox business was inevitable, and the early thinking was to gradually allow this in non-competing lines of business, with the Xerox business having the dominant stake, say 70 per cent. This gradual shift in the business profile of partners calls for openness and trust between the company and the partners. Understanding of the financial compulsions of the partners and trust in their commitment to the Xerox business is very necessary at this stage. A higher degree of maturity in partner management is called for.

It is only natural to assume that with the passage of time, the partners would grow in strength and capabilities and their retention would need a higher degree of partner orientation within the Xerox management team. Partner management would need to evolve into a collaborative mode. From the discussions I have had with many OSAs, I believe that Xerox did not evolve in its partner management approaches.

On the contrary, I was given to understand that at the ground level, the approach was often take it or leave it. The caring of the past had abruptly given way to an authoritarian approach. In a collaborative mode, the emphasis needed to shift to transparency and an equal concern for the partners' financial health and the need for delivering results. The platform that had been set for the OSA programme would have allowed this approach and would have found strong resonance within the partner community. Unfortunately, a climate of distrust was created, at the ground level and arbitrariness set in. Absence of structured review processes and field visits by the leadership team only compounded this downwards slide.

B. The Impact of New Policies

Policy changes take place from time to time and are a natural feature in the evolution of any programme. These changes can sometimes involve major restructuring of the programme at the field level and may need careful roll-out and copious communication and support to the partners. Xerox went through a few major changes that called for this care and diligence in roll-out. The first was the transfer of ownership of the machines and therefore customers to the partners under the ASP arrangement, and the other was the consolidation of partners and the introduction of a major player such as Godrej.

The transfer of ownership of the machines to the partners involved sale of the existing debt to the partners. This proved a major deterrent, as a fair proportion of the debt was non-collectable and accumulated over the years. Passing on this debt to partners is placing a huge burden on them. This led to many partners dropping out of the Xerox fold and in the process, taking away significant number of machines and customers. It may have been in Xerox's long-term interest to offer relief to the partners on bad debts and to take on the burden themselves. This calls for vision and foresight that must be expected of reputed multinational companies.

Consolidation of partners is a natural process. A company needs to aid such consolidation and enable the new partnership to stabilise and grow. If the partners are left to their own, to forge these alliances, there could be difficulties. Mature hand-holding and guidance at this stage is mandatory for the long-term success of these alliances. In some instances, the local managers felt threatened by attempts of the service partners to unite and put huddles before such partnerships.

Guidance was needed as these partners had started their businesses as first-time entrepreneurs and built their companies very independently. Alliances calls for establishing clear roles and responsibilities and the letting go of some aspects of control. The same situation entrepreneurs face when their operations grow beyond their ability to run the company effectively, resulting in the need to induct professional managers.

Guidance on the induction of financial partners would also have been necessary. A partner network of the kind put into place by the OSA programme calls for such hand-holding. If one wonders why this is necessary and should this not be solely the responsibility of the partners, one needs to appreciate the cost of partner attrition and therefore the responsibility of the company to work for the success of alliances. This effort may have avoided the need for bringing in a partner such as Godrej and then seeing them exit the business in just over a year.

The cost of this introduction was a further loss of partners and significant machines and customers to Godrej and Xerox. The losses to Xerox can be understood from the unofficial figures of the drop in Technical Service Fees, which Xerox used to collect from its partners, from Rs 7.5 crores in 2006 to just about Rs 1.75 crores in 2012. The loss on account of future business opportunity with lost customers can only be surmised.

The introduction of Godrej in Delhi and Mumbai is a case study in itself. The business plan discussed with Godrej never materialised, in terms of revenue and profitability. The people transferred to Godrej from among the Xerox managers were not the ones who could be entrusted with these responsibilities. The national manager, transferred from Xerox to Godrej for this business line, was a person who was being offered a voluntary severance.

Godrej in turn put in place large resources, including call centres and large office spaces at each location, mobile vans for spares support, and a managerial team that more or less matched what Xerox may have had, prior to the introduction of Godrej. This was untenable at the profit margins available in the business. Further the burden of bad debts transferred to them, investments in spares and consumables, and the losses of machines to exiting OSAs, all added to the financial woes of Godrej and to their inevitable exit from the business.

Short-term actions have long-term repercussions and need to be planned and executed with care. In the case of the introduction of Godrej, one can see that such planning and care was not taken. It seemed as if the programme managers were working on a deadline and chose to close the deal without adequate consideration of the future repercussions.

The loss of a partner such as Godrej in such a short period of time is a poor reflection on the programme managers in Xerox. If indeed Xerox believed its interests would have been served better with a large and financial strong partner such as Godrej, it should have done much more to ensure success of the partnership. Failure would be too costly, and this has actually turned out to be the case.

C. The 8-Stage Process for Leading Change—Kotter

Dr John Kotter is a leading authority on leading and managing change. I have selected his popular and highly rated 8-Stage Process as the theoretical foundation for planning and executing change in organizations and examining our approach to the launch of the OSA Programme.

Kotter's 8-Stages are:

Establish a sense of urgency

A key enabler for creating a sense of urgency and acceptance is to communicate messages that aim for the heart. Data heavy and analytical messages reach the head but do not influence the heart. I believe we had succeeded in reaching the hearts of our team; not just those who opted to be outsource partners but also those who were responsible for running the programme.

Creating the guiding coalition

Putting together the right coalition of people to lead a change initiative is critical to its success. That coalition must have the right composition, a significant level of trust, and a shared objective. This is possibly one of the most critical requirements. The right composition of the coalition that guides change has the ability to reach to large constituencies through informal influence and role modeling.

The team we put together to champion the programme was appropriate and performed their responsibilities very well. This is clearly a major reason for the early success after we launched the programme.

Developing a change vision

A clear vision enables a simple and understandable view of the strategies of the company. It also motivates people to take action in the right direction even if the first steps are painful. It helps to coordinate the actions of different people who clearly understand what is required of them. A clear and powerful vision will do far more than an authoritarian decree or micromanagement can ever hope to accomplish.

We did establish a clear and acceptable vision at the launch of the programme. Copious communication across all stake holders and the customer service team helped us. There is always room for improvement in communication exercises of this nature and there were certainly gaps in our programme communication. However in retrospect the communication was reasonably good.

Empowering broad based action

Kotter calls for removal of all organization barriers that can hind performance and be a drag on change management initiatives. This is an aspect that may be over looked as managers remain myopic to the institutional causes of under performance.

In addition, a barrier to effective change can be troublesome supervisors. These managers have agendas of their own that inhibits change. They may not actively undermine the effort, but they are simply not "wired" to go along with what the change requires. Such supervisors need to be addressed very quickly to either get them to change dysfunctional behavior or move on.

Generating short term wins

Short term wins provide evidence that the sacrifices that people are making are paying off. This increases the sense of urgency and the optimism of those who are making the effort to change. These wins also serve to reward the change agents by providing positive feedback that boosts morale and motivation. The wins also serve the practical purpose of helping to fine tune the vision and the strategies. The guiding coalition gets important information that allows them to course-correct.

We had employed a set of initiatives that would recognize good work done by the OSAs and show case their effort besides rewarding them. These included participation in Gland slam recognition events, participation in SMWG Conventions and other national meets, and also high visibility communication on Customer Satisfaction results. The CSMS results were a very visible recognition of the good work being put in by several of the OSAs and good results were very gratifying for the programme team.

Never letting up

Leadership is necessary to make change stick. Instead of declaring victory and moving on leaders need to launch more and more projects to drive the change deeper into the organization. They will also take the time to ensure that all the new practices are firmly grounded in the organization's culture. Managers, by their nature, think in shorter time frames. It is up to leaders to steer the course for the long-term.

This is an area that may have been over looked in subsequent developments of the OSA programme over the last decade since its launch.

Incorporating change into culture

Changing well entrenched organization cultures is exceedingly difficult and is rightfully placed as the last stage in the change process. Proof that the new way is yielding results is necessary. New norms and values need to be reinforced with incentives and rewards.

Over all it may not be an exaggeration if we claim that even Kotter may have had a few appreciative nods for the manner in which we launched this programme that involved such a disruptive change within our team.

7. IN HINDSIGHT

In hindsight, the OSA programme has given to many Xerox customer service employees a wonderful platform to build a business of their own. The successful ones have applied their training at Xerox and business acumen to establish a sustainable and profitable business model.

The OSA programme was very dear to my heart, and I always wished for success for the intrepid early adopters. I was so very happy to talk to some of them in the course of writing this book and documenting their stories. I do feel a sense of fulfilment and satisfaction, as I look back at the programme over the last decade, and I am happy that it has worked out well for so many of them, whether they have remained in Xerox's fold or moved on.

It is disappointing to see how changes in programme management approach within Xerox have adversely affected the possible benefits to the company. However, this is a matter that is best judged by the present stakeholders of the company from the standpoint of the company's strategic directions and objectives of the programme.

The stories narrated here, I am sure, would have served as wonderful reference material for aspiring entrepreneurs. They bring out the creative opportunities that entrepreneurship offers and the richer balance between work and family. Readers would not have missed the overall feeling of accomplishment, in most of the stories, and the high engagement in social activities.

A. Managing Service Outsourcing

The experiences of the early adopters brings out some concerns on effective management of outsource programmes and how certain behaviours and attitudes can result in setbacks to the programme.

Here are some of the basic ingredients for a successful service outsourcing initiative. I speak here mainly of the transition from a direct service model to an outsource partner-led model; however, many of these ideas hold good for service outsourcing in general.

* Select your partners carefully. Employees who have displayed enterprise and the drive to achieve results are the ones to select. Those that you wish to move out of the company as you downsize may not be the best choice.
* Allow for transparency and trust in your dealings with the partner and in the policies and expectations of the programme.
* Work for win-win solutions. Be supportive of your partners, and work for their long-term success and retention. Remember that partners lost are setbacks for the programme and result in substantial losses.
* Treat your partners with dignity and respect. Be firm in your expectations of performance and conformance to ethical standards. Be collaborative and supportive as you review their performance and help them reach higher standards of business excellence.
* Stay connected to the field realities through regular field visits and performance audits.
* Provide the enablers for success, including training, business appreciation workshops, and tools such as service management IT solutions.
* Ensure that the business planning you do, both from the perspective of the company and also from that of the partners, are sensible and fact-based. Take a long-term view as you lay down plans and strategies for the programme.

The behavioural aspects of managing service outsource programmes are very important to the success of the programme. There is a tendency for managers at the location level to be authoritarian. Outsource partners are lower in the pecking order in their assessment. The right approach is to treat partners with dignity and respect. A touch of humility and the willingness to listen and take feedback are the traits of successful programme managers.

Managing any programme involves the standard tools of programme management and also a mindset that I can only call 'spiritual'. By this I mean, honesty and sincerity of purpose in aligning the goals of the programme with the goals of the company. It is being spiritual to do the very best you can for the success of the programme and working towards creating a lasting institution of value.

Following are a few principles I value very much and believe are the foundation for successful careers, and I dare say, for a fulfilling life itself:

* Place the interests of your company and team above your own self interest.
* Align your personal goals and those of your team to the goals of your company.
* Teams that work in harmony and with empowerment, along clearly stated goals and directions, achieve much more than individual brilliance.
* Enable every member of your team to experience a sense of participation and to achieve their potential.

You may ask, how does one go about doing this? Well, every mature and successful professional knows that these are the recipe for success. Working closely with every team member and understanding how best they can contribute is a must. Articulating clearly your company's strategic directions and goals and those of your team is essential for creating a workplace that your team members will love to work in and give of their very best.

A touch of humility and the ability to take the rough and the smooth in your stride will do you a world of good.

As Rudyard Kipling wrote,

> *If you can keep your head when all about you are losing theirs and blaming it on you;*
> *If you can trust yourself when all men doubt you, but make allowance for their doubting too:*
> *If you can fill the unforgiving minute with sixty seconds' worth of distance run,*
> *Yours is the Earth and everything that's in it,*
> *And which is more; you'll be a Man, my son!*

Outsourced Service Partner Contact Details

Dogra, Kulbir

Dynamik Business Systems
SCO 84-85 Sector 17C 1st Foor
Chandigarh 160 017
Phone: +91 172 5018888, 2722622
Fax: +91 172 2720485
Mobile: +91 9815100111
kulbirdogra@dynamikbusiness.com
www.dynamikbusiness.com

Dhale,Ravi

NEXGEN NETWORK,
2103/2,E, Block 1-5, Near LIC Ground
Rukmininagar, Kolhapur (Maharashtra)
PIN 416005, Tel Fax—0231 2537994, Tel: 2530111 Mbl.09850903759
Mail id: nexfix@gmail.com

Kahlon, Jagmohan

J.M.Service Enterprises,
C/O Bhatia Complex,
Near Charan Pul,
Dari Road,
Dharamshala,
Kangra Distt. (H.P.)-176057
Jmse116@yahoo.com

Gupta, Sanjiv Kumar

Universal Engineers
Opp. K. C.Motors (Chevrolet),
Bye Pass Road, Channi Rama,
Jammu.-180015
Tel: 0191-2460272, 2460273
E mail: universal.jammu@gmail.com

Nandwani, Dinesh

Absolute Solution
SF—Dish TV India Ltd.
SCF 1, First Floor, Sanskriti Plaza,
Spring Field Colony, Sector 31,
Faridabad 121003, Haryana
E Mail: dinesh.nandwani@absolutsolution.in

Ramchandran, A

Integrated Systems,
2Subshree Apts.,
Vise Mala, BalBhate Path,
College Road,
Nasik Road, 422005.
ramchandran1901@gmail.com

Saravanan, MR

Qtech Sales & Services,
101, 24 Anna Nagar,1st Street,
Opp. Sixer Complex, Saradha College Road, Salem—636007
E mail: qtechstar@gmail.com
Web site: http//qtech.us.to
Fax: 0427-4030600

Singh, Jatinder

Quality Services
119, 2nd floor.
Super Plaza Market.
Cooper Road.
Amritsar.

Vaishnav, Prashant

Imprint Automation Services Pvt. Limited
806, 8th Floor, Wall-Street-1,
Ellisbridge,
Ahmedabad-380006
Cell: +91-9825802442
Tel/Fax: +91-79-26560952/26408396
http://www.imprintauto.com/

Sehdev, Vijay

Super Technosys,
75, Vinay Block,
Laxmi Nagar,
Vikas Marg,
New Delhi-110092
Email: sehdev_vijay@yahoo.co.uk.